SECRETS
to a
HAPPY
LIFE

SECRETS

to a

HAPPY

LIFE

Finding Satisfaction in Any Situation

Bill Giovannetti

BETHANYHOUSE

a division of Baker Publishing Group
Minneapolis, Minnesota

© Copyright 2013 by William Giovannetti

Published by Bethany House Publishers
11400 Hampshire Avenue South
Bloomington, Minnesota 55438
www.bethanyhouse.com

Bethany House Publishers is a division of
Baker Publishing Group, Grand Rapids, Michigan

Printed in the United States of America

Library of Congress Cataloging-in-Publication Data
Giovannetti, Bill.
    Secrets to a happy life : finding satisfaction in any situation / Bill Giovannetti.
        pages cm
    Includes bibliographical references and index.
    Summary: "A pastor shares biblical wisdom to help readers find contentment in God rather than circumstances. Includes discussion questions"—Provided by publisher.
        ISBN 978-0-7642-1124-9 (pbk. : alk. paper) 1. Happiness—Religious aspects—Christianity. 2. Contentment—Religious aspects—Christianity. I. Title.
    BV4647.J68G56 2013
    248.4—dc23   2013002678

Cover design by Dan Pitts

Author is represented by Books & Such Literary Agency

13 14 15 16 17 18 19   7 6 5 4 3 2 1

For Josie and J.D.
You make me happy by being yourselves.

For Margi
Your smile is all I need.

Contents

Contents

Introduction

God Is Happy

We all desire to be happy. That is something that is innate in human nature; nobody wants to be miserable, though I am aware of the fact that there are people who seem to enjoy being miserable and some who seem to find their happiness in being unhappy![1]

—D. Martyn Lloyd-Jones

I can't dance.

Whatever muscles are supposed to swivel my hips seized up decades ago. My sense of rhythm puts me in a league with tambourine-wielding preschoolers. And the closest thing I have to *moves* looks like the human equivalent of a cat hacking up fur balls.

In my mid-twenties, I sat at a wedding reception, hanging out with friends. A young woman approached me to dance. I didn't know her; I was sure my soon-to-be-ex-friends put her up to it. My ears turned blazing hot, my face turned red, and I said, "No thanks."

Miss Dance-a-lot didn't like that answer. She grabbed my arm and started pulling me onto the dance floor.

I panicked.

"Um, no thanks," I said, voice quavering like a scared ten-year-old's.

"Come on! It'll be fun."

Music pounded. Lights flashed. Bodies moved. Sweat poured. I refused. All I could think of was the humiliation of a crowd of people watching me wiggle my body in ways it doesn't know how to wiggle, with a woman I didn't know.

I did the only thing I could.

I held on to my chair. The flirt dragged the chair, with me in it, about ten feet, digging a nice scratch into the shiny hardwood floor. My friends laughed so hard liquid spewed from their nostrils.

God will repay them.

I wanted to die. The disco lights hypnotized me. The girl clawed at me. I clamped a death grip on my chair, figuring if we were going to dance, there were going to be four extra legs involved.

By the time we scraped our way twelve feet, my new main squeeze gave up and skulked away.

Thank God.

The floor remains scratched and my soul remains scarred.

I am sure plenty of dance instructors will read this and think they can work their magic on me. Put some hip-hop into this dance-challenged geek; woo me with their ballroom floor charts and do-si-dos.

Not going to happen.

Because, aside from the fact my body is physically incapable of the sultry moves on *Dancing with the Stars,* my deep-seated emotions long ago placed dancing on permanent lockdown.

I can't dance because I had it drummed into my head as a kid that dancing was a sin. God frowned on it as "a vertical expression of a horizontal desire."

That anti-dance brainwashing was part of a larger religious package. No movies, no drinking, no card-playing, no drums, no holding hands with the opposite sex, no . . . if you've seen *Footloose,* you get the picture.

Excessive fun was taboo.

Why?

Because God was not to be trifled with, and he was most pleased when I was most unhappy. At the core of my young faith squatted the ogres of self-denial, self-abasement, and self-sacrifice. Too much happiness was a sin, and self-interest was the root of all evil.

My religious upbringing offered an odd combination of good and bad, love and condemnation—"the best of times and the worst of times." I'm grateful for it, but there was a lot of unlearning to do.

Especially in the happiness department.

I had to learn that in the plan of God, unhappiness was not a virtue. I'm sure some readers are already saying, "Duh." Bear with me, because a whole lot of people need to be delivered from the delusion that God is the Lord of Party Pooping.

God is happy. God is not miserable. He doesn't have bad days. Isn't moody.

Heaven is a party God throws for everyone who wants in on the action. Complete with dancing—Jesus said so (Luke 15:25).

God wants you to be happy. He designed you to seek happiness like a moth seeks light.

C. S. Lewis wrote, "If there lurks in most modern minds the notion that to desire our own good and earnestly hope for the enjoyment of it is a bad thing, I submit that this notion . . . is no part of the Christian faith."[2]

True.

God wants you happy, and, if you walk his path, you can be happy.

You can even bust a move.

An old-time preacher named Billy Sunday said, "If you have no joy, there's a leak in your Christianity somewhere." That's what I'm talking about.

When I imagined God unhappy, life made me unhappy.

But when I began to see the joy of God and the pleasures of heaven, I found myself tapping in to satisfying springs of happiness. I even found my toes tapping to God's music.

I confess I am a happy man.

So what if I still can't dance!

If you're ready for the life-changing secrets, just turn the page.

What Is Happiness?

I do not depend for my happiness upon what is happening
to me. My life, my happiness, my joy and my experience
are independent of the things that are going on about me,
and even of the things that may be happening to me. . . .[1]

—D. Martyn Lloyd-Jones

Surface Happiness

Let's think of happiness on two levels: surface happiness and
deep happiness.

Surface happiness refers to everyday pleasures that bring us
joy. It is happiness based on happenings. When circumstances
are good, I feel happy. When my wife laughs at the joke I've been
saving up for her, that's happiness—especially after a string of
duds that got me the dreaded wifely eye-roll. When my kid nails
the piano recital and blows a kiss to Mom as the final notes drift
into musical legendom, that's happiness. When my friends devour
the chicken cacciatore and beg for the recipe, that's happiness.

We live for moments like these.

And yet, they're fickle. The same daughter who blew the kiss
at a recital will stomp away in a queenly snit over the wrong icing

on the cake. The mother-in-law who loved the chicken will make a snide remark over your eldest son's manners.

In those moments, surface happiness pops like a soap bubble, and the festive family affair collapses into a fighting match. Even though it doesn't have much staying power, surface happiness is still a good thing. The Bible puts a stamp of approval on it, calling God the one "who gives us richly all things to enjoy" (1 Timothy 6:17).

Even so, the happiness born of wealth and fame—the happiness of celebrities and athletes whose faces adorn the tabloids—will never be enough, because surface happiness depends on *circumstances*. Was the lasagna hot enough? Did I exercise enough? Did my kids have a good day? Did enough money come in to pay the bills? Did the plastic surgery look good?

Maybe yes, maybe no.

When surface happiness is out of reach, then what?

That's when it's time for a happiness that goes clear to the bones.

Deep Happiness

If surface happiness is like the waves rolling onto a beach, deep happiness would be like the strong ocean currents. Though we do not see them, deep currents traverse the world's oceans with a force sixteen times stronger than all the world's rivers combined.[2] The surface can be calm or choppy—it doesn't matter. The deep currents just keep flowing.

That's the happiness we're after.

This deep happiness shows up in all kinds of ways. It can be excited, such as when I'm on my feet cheering my son's touchdown. It can be quiet, such as when I'm sitting on the back deck over coffee, taking in forested valleys and snow-capped peaks. Deep happiness flows in any situation because it is anchored beyond circumstances. Even tears on the outside can't detour the current of joy on the inside.

Deep happiness flows from God.

That's what this book is about, and that's why we're scouring the Bible for the ingredients to happiness.

Doesn't it make sense to check your Maker's instruction manual if you want the joy he designed you for?

It is possible you picked up this book without a belief in God. Perhaps, for you, God is a higher power. Or a spiritual force. Or a myth. I promise not to cram God down your throat—but you will see that this book is written from a perspective that God is real, and that the happy life is ultimately a God-blessed life.

Whether you accept the God-premise or not, I invite you to consider this book your invitation to a quest for deep happiness—an abiding contentment that money can't buy, failed liposuction can't remove, and bankers can't repossess.

Being Content No Matter What

Over 350 years ago, while Pilgrims braved the seas, Puritan pastor Jeremiah Burroughs offered this classic definition: "Christian contentment is that sweet, inward, quiet, gracious frame of spirit, which freely submits to and delights in God's wise and fatherly disposal in every condition."[3]

I like this definition. Let's work with it.

Burroughs recognized a secret few mortals discover: *Happiness begins in the soul.* It starts inside me, in my beliefs, attitudes, instincts, and feelings.

The eleven secrets of a happy life aren't about splashy surface waves, but subsurface determinants of your whole way of being. They are eleven secrets tied together by a single conviction: an unshakable belief in God's "wise and fatherly disposal" in each condition. In this book, I want to help redirect the deep currents in your soul.

I can't wave a magic wand and make you happy. No human can—no matter what they promise or what gimmicks they peddle—and God won't.

But I can promise a journey. And I do have a map—it's the bittersweet story of a man who found deep happiness a million miles away from where he thought he would. His name was Joseph—of the *Amazing Technicolor Dreamcoat* fame.

Three millennia have slipped by since Joseph's days, yet his story is more popular than ever: Over 20,000 performances of the famous Andrew Lloyd Webber play have been performed all over the English-speaking world. Think about it: The three-thousand-year-old story of a Jewish man in Egypt's courts is sung and danced in the English-speaking world. Why?

Because in this difficult world, the search for happiness never grows old.

Happiness U

In the 1960s, researchers at Stanford University studied delayed gratification in four-year-olds. They put a marshmallow in front of the kids and gave them two choices. Choice one: Eat it now. Choice two: Wait twenty minutes and receive an extra marshmallow.

Researchers then followed these four-year-olds all the way to college. The kids who delayed their marshmallow gratification—who waited at age four—were better adjusted as teenagers, were more dependable in school, and scored an average 210 points higher on their SATs than their confection-inhaling peers.[4]

Many people approach their deep character traits, like maturity and happiness, as some four-year-olds approach a marshmallow. *Gimme, gimme, gimme. Now!*

Contrast that spirit with Saint Paul's confession: "I have learned in whatever state I am, to be content" (Philippians 4:11).

He *learned* contentment. God didn't reach down and inject him with it. Paul underwent a process. He grew up.

That's why I'm not offering suggestions about more quality time with your kids, or time management, or *fêng shui* for your living room. Our culture offers all kinds of resources for surface happiness.

Sooner or later, however, you have to dig deep. You need principles, not techniques; values, not tips. You have to radically reform your root beliefs. You have to launch your quest.

You picked up this book for a reason. Your time is now.

It's time to begin the journey.

It's time to redirect the deep ocean currents.

Let's learn from a master of deep happiness, a man who suffered greatly and stood at the end of his days bloodied but unbowed—Joseph, son of Jacob, a deeply happy man.

It's time to lift the veil on the first secret of happiness.

FOR REFLECTION AND DISCUSSION

1. Would you say your friends are more dependent on surface happiness or deep happiness?

2. What makes you happy? Unhappy?

3. Would you say that you and your family are basically happy? Is it more of a surface happiness or a deep happiness?

4. What role does God play in a person's happiness? Do you think most of your friends connect the dots between God and their happiness on a regular basis? Do you?

5. What does Psalm 37:4 say about a person's deep happiness?

Secret

#1

--- # Letting Go ---

The houses we live in, the homes we love, the riches we accumulate, the professions we follow, the plans we form, the relations we enter into, they are only for a time. The things you live for now are all temporary and passing away. . . . They are poor ephemeral things which cannot last. Oh, do not love them too much! Do not grasp them too tightly! Do not make them your idols! You cannot keep them, and you must leave them!

—J. C. Ryle

* * *

A Pilgrim's Heart

Think like a pilgrim, holding all things lightly,
because earth's deepest joys are rooted
in heaven's highest blessing.

* * *

The blood trickling from the boy's ear was nothing compared to the flood rushing from the gash over his right eye. An egg-sized lump had already formed. As he regained consciousness, confusion gave way to panic. *How long have I been here?*

Bones in his left forearm crunched as he struggled against the bonds that squeezed his hands and feet. Useless.

Faint light from an opening above let him survey his surroundings. Nothing but spiderwebs, scorpions, loose rocks, and dirt. And a teenage kidnap victim, straining against his bonds.

Why me? Why would they attack me? What will they do?

"Help! Somebody, please help!"

His scratchy voice echoed against hard walls. For a moment silence reigned. Then he heard them. From a distance. They had heard his plea, and they responded, "Help! Please help! I'm so scared!" They mimicked his cry, taunting him.

The boy heard his would-be killers laugh.

Pressing his head against the ground, he closed his eyes and did the only thing he could do.

He prayed.

And finally, he slept.

Hours later—or was it days?—he awoke to the sound of voices above. A rope snaked from the opening, landing on the rock floor beside him. One of his captors descended hand over hand.

The boy hunched in a corner, shivering from hypothermia, weary from dehydration. Bloodied. Soiled. Beaten. He saw the knife in his captor's sheath. His heart raced. He told himself he was ready. He'd made his peace. He was finished fighting.

His only prayer . . . *Lord, make it fast.*

The mangled teenager lying at the bottom of that pit was destined to rule the known world. He had no clue of the epic happiness just ahead. He only knew that his own brothers hated him, and his life had taken a sudden turn toward the dark side.

At this point, Joseph seems like an unlikely role model for happiness, but let's stick with him. His whole life is a clinic on clinging to God's goodness in tough times.

There's a powerful scene in *The Call of the Wild*, with John Thornton sitting at the edge of a three-hundred-foot cliff. He's joined by two friends and his faithful dog, Buck. Buck is a cross-breed between a Saint Bernard and a collie. He's fiercely loyal to his master, and John Thornton knows it.

But he wants to test it.

A thoughtless whim seized Thornton, and he drew the attention of Hans and Pete to the experiment he had in mind. "Jump, Buck!" he commanded, sweeping his arm out and over the chasm. The next instant he was grappling with Buck on the extreme edge, while Hans and Pete were dragging them back to safety.

"It's uncanny," Pete said, after it was over and they had caught their speech.

Thornton shook his head. "No, it is splendid, and it is terrible, too. Do you know, it sometimes makes me afraid."[1]

It made him afraid because the fierceness of Buck's devotion demanded an equal and greater devotion from his master—and John Thornton wasn't sure he could unfailingly supply it. What decent person would abuse a trust so deep? It's unthinkable, don't you think?

Yet every day, countless people shrink back from the joyful life God calls them to because they think low thoughts of their Master. They fear he will abuse their faith. He will make them jump the cliff for no good reason.

Could it be we harbor the suspicion that our God is randomly seized with "thoughtless whims" like John Thornton?

If God swept his arm and told you, "Jump!" would you look at him like he's crazy? Would you measure the distance to impact, calculate terminal velocity, and negotiate alternatives first?

Yeah, me too.

That's why I'm writing this book.

Because no one's happiness rises above their trust in God, and no one's trust rises above their conception of him. I want to scrape off the crud that's accumulated on your God-concept. I want to unleash a big God worthy of a big trust. I want a God who isn't random and doesn't act on whim—a God who has a mind-blowingly beautiful plan, and who, like a good-hearted big brother, includes me in it. If he says jump, there's a reason better than any I can imagine, even if I don't know it yet.

I want to be confident in him enough to jump the cliff if he says so.

You?

Pilgrims

Joseph faced shocking adversity. Undeserved. Irrational. Vindictive. Evil. He fell prey to hardships that would make the Incredible Hulk curl up in a fetal position and beg for Mommy.

But he stood strong in God.

For Joseph, adversity was inevitable but misery was optional. He couldn't control what other people did to him, but he could control his reactions. For those reactions, he tapped in to secret powers beyond this world and found happiness that transcended life's horrendous circumstances.

We will follow his story in the Bible to garner our secrets to happiness. His story is not the only place in the Bible we'll look—there'll be some detours. But the Joseph-epic will be our main road.

Even if you're not a God-person or a Bible lover, I encourage you to stay with me; maybe you'll learn something about happiness. Plus, it never hurts to have your preconceptions challenged.

For Joseph, happiness wasn't about a menu of techniques or a collection of problem-solving solutions. It was about living daily before an almighty God who gripped him in the palm of his hand.

Let's jump into the story.

The first factoid in Joseph's profile reveals a very basic secret of his happiness.

Now Jacob lived in the land where his father had sojourned, in the land of Canaan. These are the records of the generations of Jacob. Joseph, when seventeen years of age, was pasturing the flock with his brothers while he was still a youth, along with the sons of Bilhah and the sons of Zilpah, his father's wives. And

Joseph brought back a bad report about them to their father. Now Israel loved Joseph more than all his sons, because he was the son of his old age; and he made him a varicolored tunic.

Genesis 37:1–3 NASB

To sojourn means to live as a pilgrim. Joseph was a sojourner from a long line of sojourners. His family saw themselves as permanent travelers, strangers, and aliens. When you see yourself as a pilgrim, you define yourself as a temporary resident in an alien land. You don't sink roots. You don't build houses. You camp out in tents, hold all things lightly, and are ready to go at a moment's notice.

To begin the epic of Joseph, the author, Moses, zoomed in on the detail that . . .

- Joseph's father, Jacob, was a pilgrim (Genesis 47:9);
- Joseph's grandfather, Isaac, was a pilgrim (Genesis 37:1); and
- Joseph's great-grandfather, Abraham, was a pilgrim too (Genesis 17:8–9).

Now it was Joseph's turn. Whatever wealth heaven dropped into his lap, whatever places he owned, whatever nations bowed before him, in the end, Joseph never forgot his true status in this world: Planet earth was not his home; he was just passing through.

Do you see yourself as a pilgrim?

No matter how much wealth you have or don't have, you're just passing through. It's one thing to say it. It's another thing to believe it.

Disclaimer: You can't just pick up a book and *decide* to have a pilgrim heart, any more than you can *decide* to cook a ten-course Italian feast without working your way up to it. A pilgrim's heart is an attitude you *cultivate*, over time, through spirituality, Scripture, prayer, and tough choices.

Your happiness will always be at risk unless you detach your safety lines from earthly possessions and reattach them to riches in heaven that nothing can destroy.

23

When you read *pilgrim* you might think of hopping on the *Mayflower* and churning your own butter in a log cabin in the new world. But the biblical concept predates American pilgrims by several thousand years. Here are three basic attitudes to cultivate if you want to be a modern-day pilgrim. Consider them marching orders for a deeply happy heart.

Detachment

> By faith Abraham obeyed when he was called to go out to the place which he would receive as an inheritance. And he went out, not knowing where he was going.
>
> Hebrews 11:8

Start with the attitude of healthy *detachment*. I'm not talking about hating the world, or becoming a hermit or a monk. I'm talking about not getting your emotions deeply entwined with your stuff, or your success, or your security, or your earthly resources.

This is hard.

The attitude of detachment swims upstream against the flow of our society.

Have you ever considered the possibility that our materialistic culture is 180 degrees out of phase with reality? What if we've been brainwashed into materialism? If truth is reality as God sees it, then reality says our primary relationship is with God. Every other relationship comes in second place or lower—especially our relationship with *stuff*.

Our problem, however, starts with the simple fact that our bond with God is weak. Our hearts abhor a vacuum, so we bond with lesser things. We fill our dance card with other partners. Over time we grow fond of them. Affection for life's stuff crowds out affection for God. When God invites us to love him with our *whole* heart, we answer back, "As soon as I'm done decorating the house."

True pilgrims practice the art of healthy detachment. They hold all things lightly and love nothing and no one more than God.

Some time ago my family and I moved from the urban jungle of Chicago to the mountains and lakes of northern California.

We felt like the Beverly Hillbillies, with moving vans and cars filled with stuff. In the move, we decided to leave behind our woodworking gear. My wife, Margi, and I loved building things together. We weren't experts at it, but we built some cool projects. We sold off our table saw, drill press, oscillating spindle sander, surface planer, jointer, clamps, band saw, and a basement full of hand tools and power tools.

We sold off a pile of antique barnwood and scraps of quality hardwood.

I like to think I'm as manly as the next guy, but I might have squeezed off a tear or two as I watched my equipment go. Over a decade later, and from two thousand miles away, I still miss my rock-solid Atlas drill press.

God had to peel my fingers off some stuff that brought me happiness so he could bring me to a place of greater happiness. It's part of life.

Whatever you have, enjoy it while you have it, and don't go psycho when you have to let it go.

Consider Joseph's great-grandfather, Abram. One sunny afternoon, Abram (soon to be called Abraham) was mowing his lush lawn, whistling country music, and anticipating dinner with Sarai (soon to be called Sarah), his intelligent and beautiful wife. His face lit up as he surveyed his white picket fence, his four-camel garage, and his executive mansion overlooking his own Ponderosa.

Out of the clear blue sky, God spoke to him:

> Now the LORD had said to Abram: "Get out of your country, from your family and from your father's house, to a land that I will show you. I will make you a great nation; I will bless you and make your name great; and you shall be a blessing. I will bless those who bless you, and I will curse him who curses you; and in you all the families of the earth shall be blessed."
>
> Genesis 12:1–3

One moment he was living the dream, and the next moment, God waved his arm in an unspecified direction and said *"Jump!"*

What would you have said? "God, you don't understand. I have bills to pay, and we specifically moved here for the schools. Plus, Sarai just ordered new flooring. . . . We'll be on hardwood next week! I just can't up and go. I need details. Where should I go? What is the route? Why am I going there? Is my next job lined up? Please, God. Be reasonable."

If Abram proves anything, he proves that God's idea of unreasonable isn't the same as ours. He expects in you a kind of detachment that can just get up and go.

Can you pray, "Go ahead, God, move me. Change my job. Change my health. Change my finances. Change my home. Change my surroundings. You can throw me in a pit, in a prison, or in a palace. It doesn't matter. It will not spoil my deep-level joy, because my joy is not anchored in this temporal world. I'm a pilgrim. If you say jump, I'll take the leap"?

How white are your knuckles? How much do you freak out over your kids' grades, your carpet's cleanliness, the economy, money, or the house? How much misery have you created over your losses? Your fears of diseases that might strike or of wars that might happen? Or of conspiracies that might unfold?

It's a mistake to anchor your happiness to anything kids can spill grape juice on, bankers can repossess, hackers can infiltrate, or fashion gurus can make passé.

Here's a little test: Let your kids (or grandkids, nieces, nephews, or church youth group) eat oversized ice-cream cones in the fanciest place in your house or car, and laugh over the mess they make.

Or have a food fight.

Unclench.

Abram uprooted his life and started moving. His familiar places, favorite restaurants, and a lifetime of friends receded in the rearview mirror.

Bye-bye, safe, comfortable, familiar life.

Hello, adventure.

And God pointed the way, one footfall at a time. Healthy detachment.

Simplicity

By faith [Abram] dwelt in the land of promise as in a foreign country, dwelling in tents with Isaac and Jacob, the heirs with him of the same promise.

Hebrews 11:9

Yes, I said our main story is about Joseph, yet we're still hovering around his great-grandparents, Abraham and Sarah. Here's why: Their DNA flowed through Joseph's veins.

When they got to where God led them, Abraham and Sarah pitched a tent and called it good. They were a power-couple, among the wealthiest of their day, but they lived in a tent. I'm sure it was a very nice tent, but it was still a tent.

So what?

Your healthy detachment needs to go along with *happy simplicity*. Scripture records no permanent dwellings for the first three generations of the Jews: Abraham, Isaac, or Jacob. And don't miss the important little detail that Abram and Sarah had already made it to the Promised Land; they were in their official God-given, earthly home, yet they still lived in tents.

Why?

Because not even the earthly Promised Land was the finish line. For Abraham and Sarah, the finish line did not exist on planet earth. They saw life as a journey to heaven.

The early Christians knew this. Peter advised, "Beloved, I beg you as sojourners and pilgrims, abstain from fleshly lusts which war against the soul" (1 Peter 2:11). Be a pilgrim, he said. Don't get weighed down by fleshly lusts—by all the pleasures that promise happiness but never deliver.

Last summer our family took our first-ever trip to Disneyland. Two adults, two kids, five suitcases, four backpacks, pillows, water bottles, snacks . . . I felt like a pack animal lugging all that stuff to our hotel room. We told ourselves to pack light. Somehow, in the process, we convinced ourselves we *needed* more than we did.

By the end of our trip to the happiest place on earth, we had left untouched over half of what we packed.

I was embarrassed.

Jesus warned that we can choke out our happiness through "cares, riches, and pleasures [*hedone*, in Greek] of life" (Luke 8:14). Good pilgrims carry light backpacks.

A simplified life creates margin. Time to breathe. Time for unhurried conversation with your spouse. Time to build a Star Wars Lego cruiser with your son, and to read Nancy Drew mysteries with your daughter. Surplus money to buy coffee for a street person, dig wells in Asia, take in a movie with your spouse, and help build a hospital in Africa.

Simplicity.

Without it, you no longer run your life. Your overcrowded calendar app runs your life. Your obscene mountain of possessions crammed into your garage, basement, and rented storage units runs your life. Looking for stuff you know you have but can't find because it's crammed into closets and drawers runs your life. The debt you incurred buying all that stuff runs your life. Your jangled emotions, hopped up on adrenaline or dampened down by narcotics, run your life.

Like a fly hopelessly tangled in a spider's web, you've been snared by too many commitments, too many possessions, and too many complications.

Simplify.

Have a garage sale, and give the money to orphans. Get rid of your storage units. Downsize early.

Abraham and Sarah were the Donald and Ivanka Trumps of their generation. They could have built a palace, but they lived in tents.

Attachment

For he waited for the city which has foundations, whose builder and maker is God.

Hebrews 11:10

Before I owned a house, I lived in a tiny apartment. I called that basement apartment home for ten years in urban Chicago.

I lived paycheck to paycheck as a young, single pastor, and was sure I'd never own a home.

One Christmas season, a pastor friend joined me for lunch. I drove. Wayne led a small church and he lived in a modest house with his awesome family.

For lunch, we traveled into a wealthy suburban town to a barbecue joint. We were two broke pastors driving through a rich neighborhood at Christmas.

We looked at those beautiful mansions, sparkling with decorations, sprinkled with enough snow to look like Norman Rockwell paintings. We both got very quiet.

We were jealous.

We were depressed.

We drove by a particularly ornate home. A mansion.

We paused.

That's when Wayne—always a wise mentor—broke the silence. "My mansion in heaven is bigger than that."

The lights came on. *Yes. I've got a mansion. In heaven. This world isn't all there is.*

Suddenly, we were content. We detached our emotional state from earth and reattached it to heaven. For that shining moment, we were happy.

When you think like a pilgrim, you realize life's ultimate rewards are future.

Jesus counseled us to lay up treasures in heaven (Matthew 6:20).

James asked, "What is your life?" He then answered, saying it is just "a vapor that appears for a little time and then vanishes away" (James 4:14). Your real home is heaven. You have seventy, eighty, maybe ninety years here, and then an eternity in heaven.

You won't be bringing any big-screen TVs, cars, boats, or high-fashion purses with you. If you can feel it, touch it, or see it now, you're going to kiss it good-bye.

Pilgrims know that.

Am I trying to be a planet-earth party pooper? Is this whole pilgrim teaching a plot to shame away the pleasures of earthly possessions? Is this my early anti-dancing upbringing rearing its spoilsport-ish head?

No.

I'm simply trying to set the pleasures of earthly possessions into a bigger context, because that context will save you a whole lot of grief when your earthly possessions malfunction or go the way of disco.

So go ahead and enjoy your home, your boat, your pool, your car, and your shiny jewelry if you have them. Just don't white-knuckle it. You need the mind-set to say even if it were to all go away, you can still be happy because your happiness reaches deeper than your stuff.

A City With Foundations

> By faith [Abraham] dwelt in the land of promise as in a foreign country, dwelling in tents with Isaac and Jacob, the heirs with him of the same promise; for he waited for the city which has foundations, whose builder and maker is God.
>
> Hebrews 11:9–10

Planet earth will always be a "foreign country" to a person who follows God. The biggest home on the block is nothing but a tent on steroids. A coming cosmic storm will blow it all away. God invites you to a celestial city. This world is not your home; you're just passing through.

Let's start here. None of the upcoming secrets to happiness will work until you unclench your happiness muscles from their Gollum-like grip on earthly delights.

You don't have to give it all away. You don't have to be ashamed of your riches. You don't need a vow of poverty or an Amish conversion.

Just hold your stuff lightly.

You have an eternity to play with.

Think like a pilgrim.

It's the only way you'll be happy. It's the only way you'll be ready to jump.

30

For Reflection and Discussion

1. How weird or not weird is the idea of being a modern-day pilgrim? How common is that thought?

2. If your kids were to describe your relationship to material possessions, what would they say? How about in relation to your relationship with God?

3. Describe a time when you worked hard to get something you really wanted, and then discovered it wasn't worth the effort.

4. Can you name some ways you can simplify your life? How will you feel?

5. What does Jesus say about laying up treasures in Matthew 6:19–21? What do you think it means?

Destiny

We are made for larger ends than Earth can encompass.
Oh, let us be true to our exalted destiny.

—Catherine Booth
(co-founder of the Salvation Army)

* * *

A Sense of Destiny
Nurture your personal sense of destiny,
because it toughens you against the storms of life.

* * *

Four boys fidgeted on metal folding chairs in an echo-filled basement of a little Chicago church. A Sunday school teacher older than Yoda and twice as wrinkled finished his lesson in a gravelly voice. He invited the boys to bow their heads for prayer. The boys wrestled their bodies into compliance, creating a rare spasm of quiet.

The old teacher, affectionately known as Uncle Ben, paused before praying. "Boys," he said, "I believe God wants some of you to serve him with your lives. Maybe God wants you to be a missionary. Maybe he's calling you to be a pastor . . ."

The words cut to the heart of at least one of those boys.

Uncle Ben continued. "Whatever it may be, perhaps God is calling you to serve him. If you think God wants you to be a pastor or missionary, raise your hand right now."

In that sacred moment, while a little boy stared at speckles on a linoleum floor of a tiny church, God swooped down and made time stand still. A powerful vision flashed across his mind. He imagined a vast arena filled with spiritually hungry people. He saw himself as a grown-up, preaching the gospel and seeing thousands of people responding to his call.

In that space-time moment, the boy knew his destiny. Though it made his heart pound, he felt embarrassed by his dream. Perhaps he knew he wasn't worthy. Perhaps he thought it was out of reach. For whatever reason, the boy determined he would never even whisper his secret.

Except to Uncle Ben.

Uncle Ben wouldn't make fun of him.

Silently, the little boy raised his hand. In that moment, God emblazoned an indelible dream across his sincere Italian heart.

I know, because I was that boy, and I was eight years old. The whole experience freaked me out. Afterward, I wanted nothing to do with it. I didn't understand it. Plus, pastors were weird, I thought. I didn't want my buddies lumping me in with them. I chalked it up to a fit of spiritual excitement and shoved the whole pastor idea on the back shelf.

But there was a problem. I couldn't shake my dream. As I wound my way through Chicago's educational system, and grown-ups began asking what I was going to do with my life, I had no answer—at least none I was willing to say out loud.

The pressure ratcheted up as it came time to choose a college and a major.

If there were an "unpastor" major, I would have signed up for it.

Fast-forward to today.

I've been in full-time pastoral ministry since age twenty. Yes, God is that funny. And, yes, a personal sense of destiny has a sneaky habit of catching up with you.

A Person of Destiny

Happy people align what they do with who they are.

You are a person of destiny. All the power of heaven conspires in your favor; God is for you (Romans 8:31). Angels protect you. Divine resources empower you. Grace inspires you. God's Spirit strengthens you. God's promises sustain you, and his strong arm upholds you.

God is infinitely more committed to you than you will ever be to him.

He has so orchestrated your corner of the cosmos that all of reality works together in your favor. Mountains crumble into the sea and demons scatter as you journey toward your destiny. You can be proud of who you become.

But you have to believe. You have to reach out for your God-given dreams. You have to press through adversity and align your outer choices with your inner dreams. This requires a mental picture of the person you long to be in your wildest dreams.

God gave me my mental picture at age eight. It was awfully nice of him to drop it on me so young. My sense of destiny arrived in a flash, like flipping on a light switch. Yours may arrive gradually, like the dawn. It makes no difference how it comes.

God may reveal it in pieces—a gentle tug toward a college major, a life-changing conversation, a short-term missions experience, an investment, an idea. As you set your shaky foot on the initial stepping-stones in that direction, your destiny will come into focus, gradually perhaps. But you will increasingly know in your heart what you were meant to be.

However it comes, your destiny is the core of your emotional DNA. You are a unique creation; you are here for a reason.

That reason keeps you going when times are hard. It motivates you to press through adversity without turning belly-up.

Part of the antidote to misery is tuning in to the deep dreams your Maker has hardwired into your personality and persevering till you achieve them.

Happy people align what they do with who they are.

Let's unearth five laws of destiny from a world-class dreamer.

The Five Laws of Destiny

*Law #1: Neither your failures nor your family's
dysfunction disqualify you from reaching
your destiny.*

Now Jacob dwelt [sojourned] in the land where his father was
a stranger, in the land of Canaan. This is the history of Jacob.
Joseph, being seventeen years old, was feeding the flock with his
brothers. And the lad was with the sons of Bilhah and the sons
of Zilpah, his father's wives; and Joseph brought a bad report
of them to his father. Now Israel loved Joseph more than all his
children, because he was the son of his old age. Also he made
him a tunic of many colors. But when his brothers saw that their
father loved him more than all his brothers, they hated him and
could not speak peaceably to him.

Genesis 37:1–4

Jacob, Joseph's very busy dad, fathered children by four different women. The kids, to put it mildly, didn't get along. Their
family tree dripped violence, incest, murder, rape, deceit, treachery, and revenge. The sons of Jacob were poster children for
dysfunction gone wild.

Enter favorite son—and runt of the family—Joseph.

Jacob assigned seventeen-year-old Joseph to oversee his gruff,
rough-and-tumble, jealous half-brothers, representing—by my
reckoning—three different mothers. These guys already hated
each other, and then two events fanned the flames of that hatred.

Event one: Jacob gave Joseph a coat of many colors. This
would be a special gift that set Joseph head and shoulders above
his gangsta brothers. Jacob loved Joseph best out of all his sons,
and he wanted all his sons to know it. The coat launched his
brothers' hatred into the stratosphere. Can't blame Jacob though.
The more you know about Joseph, the more you'll like him too.

*Event two: Joseph brought a bad report of his brothers to his
father.* Most commentaries praise Joseph for this. They suggest
the brothers did something royally bad, and Joseph did the right
thing and ratted them out.

I'm not so sure.

This part of the Bible was written in Hebrew. The word translated *report* occurs only nine times in the whole Old Testament.[1] In every other case this word means to slander somebody. It means to distort the truth in a negative or evil way.

I am sorry to fracture the fairy tale that Joseph occupied a moral pedestal above the weaknesses of the rest of us, but it is likely he slandered his brothers. Joseph was a flawed human being—like the rest of us.

And that's comforting to me, because it gives us the first law of destiny: *Neither your failures nor your family's dysfunction disqualify you from reaching your destiny.*

Let that sink in.

Here we have a monumentally messed-up family, devoted to one another's destruction, with a teenage son impacted by the family dysfunction. Yet God uses him for great good anyway.

He'll use you too. So what if you've been nothing but a mess and you come from a long line of rejects, felons, religious hypocrites, embezzlers, moochers, or addicts. Your past doesn't have to define you, because what lies behind you is never as important as what lies before you or what lies within you.

Tell me how bad your past has been and I'll tell you how great your future can be. You have a destiny, and because of what God did through Christ, failure is never fatal. Why don't you prove it? Joseph did, even as messed up as his family was.

Law #2: Your sense of destiny is God's personalized invitation to a future better than your wildest dreams.

Now Joseph had a dream, and he told it to his brothers; and they hated him even more. So he said to them, "Please hear this dream which I have dreamed: There we were, binding sheaves in the field. Then behold, my sheaf arose and also stood upright; and indeed your sheaves stood all around and bowed down to my sheaf." And his brothers said to him, "Shall you indeed reign over us? Or shall you indeed have dominion over us?" So they hated him even more for his dreams and for his words.

Genesis 37:5–8

God used dreams to permanently hardwire a vision of greatness into a young man's soul. Joseph would never forget these dreams. He could never run away from them. And no twists of history could eradicate them.

I am not using the word *destiny* in the sense that some philosophies and religions use it. In some schools of thought, destiny means fate or something like it. Your fate is written in the stars, some say. Or your fate is written in your DNA, and you really can't do anything about it. Some believe in karma, or luck, or chance, or the universe.

In ancient mythology, three blind goddesses controlled the span of every life. Commonly called the Fates, mythologists call them the *Moirae*. One goddess spun a thread, the second determined how long it would be, and the third cut it at just the right time. The Fates laughed whenever somebody tried to cheat them, because everybody knows that you can't cheat fate.

Even Zeus, the king of the gods, couldn't control them.

The biblical concept of destiny, on the other hand, flushes the Fates and their pessimistic determinism right down the toilet.

When God gave a dream to Joseph, it wasn't a fatalistic doom. It wasn't "what will be, will be."

It was a gracious invitation into a life so fantastic Joseph couldn't imagine it, so God painted the imagination on the corridors of his mind. God let Joseph taste it. For the first time in his chaotic life, a young boy, engulfed in madness, felt hope. He could stretch out a shaky hand toward a brighter tomorrow.

No matter how crazy your family was, there is hope for you today.

Hope—confidence in a promised future good—is life's best antidote to misery. Hope steels our nerves in the face of adversity. By making you believe in your tomorrows, your sense of destiny adds to your happiness today.

God birthed hope in Joseph's soul, and that is what he will do for you.

God invites you to something bigger than yourself. Something no one else can do. A life that makes you a hero to somebody—even if only in the eyes of onlooking angels and God. Even if only to a child you sacrifice for.

God didn't design you to play small. Or to keep a low profile. Or to drift. Or to fail to launch. He designed you to contribute to a great cause, bigger than this world; one that transcends time to reach into the ages of eternity.

Start praying daily for a sense of destiny and purpose in your life.

Your personal sense of destiny, like mine, may revolve around ministry. It may focus on the noble task of rearing a family. Or creating a warm and caring home. Or maybe yours revolves around a business idea. Or adopting orphans. Or teaching children, or becoming a nurse or doctor or piano teacher. Your dream may relate to prayer, medicine, finance, art, music, education, math, creating beauty, providing care, testing the limits of endurance through sports, missions, clean water, alleviating poverty, or feeding the hungry.

It may be big—healing nations, transforming societies.

It may be intimate—touching one life at a time, working behind the scenes, supporting others in their glorious quests.

Any vocation that comes from your heart becomes sacred when you pursue it for God's glory and by his strength.

Almost a thousand years after Joseph, King David would write:

Delight yourself also in the LORD, and he shall give you the desires of your heart.

Psalm 37:4

Consider this a gold-plated invitation to the desires of your heart. When your heart is good with God, your deepest desires provide a reliable guide to his will for your life. Your wants merge with his wants. I'm not talking about the little wants—I want a big-screen TV, I want a trip to Maui, I want straight teeth.

The "desires of your heart" represent your deepest wants and dreams, that vision of who you can become that seems so out of reach you're tempted to give up on it.

You can safely follow your heart because whatever desires you find there came from God.

Disclaimer: This only works when our hearts are pure, i.e., truly respectful of God and growing in the knowledge of him. If we're spiritual brats, routinely dissing God and doing our own things, our hearts turn sour and our desires only indulge our narcissism.

God is inviting you to not give up on your dreams, your hopes, your faith, your life, or your world. Today's tears water tomorrow's happiness. You have a personal invitation from God to donate your life to a great cause—one that meshes together your highest happiness and God's highest glory.

Follow your heart.

Once you catch a glimpse of God's vision for your life, you'll never be content with anything less. I know, because I tried.

Law #3: You'll never achieve your destiny if you wait for other people's approval.

Then he dreamed still another dream and told it to his brothers, and said, "Look, I have dreamed another dream. And this time, the sun, the moon, and the eleven stars bowed down to me." So he told it to his father and his brothers; and his father rebuked him and said to him, "What is this dream that you have dreamed? Shall your mother and I and your brothers indeed come to bow down to the earth before you?" And his brothers envied him, but his father kept the matter in mind.

Genesis 37:9–11

"Hey, bros, I had another dream!"
"Shut up, punk."
"Hey, Dad, I had another dream!"
Crickets.

When God confirmed my dream to be a pastor, I freaked out over what my friends would think. I imagined the schoolyard gang inflicting head noogies and humiliating wedgies. . . .

THEM: So, Bill, what are you going to be when you grow up?
ME: A pastor. And I'm going to help people get *saved*!
THEM: Hahahaha! Get him!

So, after raising my hand in Sunday school that day, I stamped CLASSIFIED over my personal sense of destiny and never told a soul. My college career—seven years, three colleges, and four majors just for a bachelor's degree—tells the story of a young man running from his dreams.

I worried what people would think, and wasted a lot of time, money, and grief in the process.

If you want to guarantee your own misery, let other people's opinions crush the life out of your dreams. That way, you can store up your frustrations and go postal a couple decades from now.

That way, you'll never hit the dance floor.

Most dreamers encounter more hecklers than cheerleaders.

If you're waiting for everyone to climb on board your bandwagon, you can count on a eulogy that begins, "A very nice person who never made waves, was liked by all, and never accomplished much, has left this world without a ripple."

That doesn't mean to ignore advice or wise counsel. It just means you should recognize that dreamers represent a threat to the world's self-satisfied underachievers.

A variation on this pursuit of other people's approval is the fear of coming across as proud, boastful, or superior. Get over that fear. Never let the people around you who have lost their dreams pull you down to their level. Don't play small. Don't play dumb. Anybody who has a dream is going to stand out.

When others say, "Who are you to think you're destined for a throne?" you need to say, "Who are you to doubt me?"

When they say, "You'll fail!" tell them, "My God never fails."

When they call you a fool, tell them, "God's foolishness is wiser than the wisdom of the world."

When they drive you from their group, run to the open arms of God.

In a famous experiment in 1967, four monkeys were placed in a cage with a banana at the top of a ladder. When a monkey headed toward the banana, researchers blasted the monkey with cold water, and blasted all the other monkeys too.[2]

After a while, all the monkeys got the message: Do not go after the banana, or else.

Researchers then swapped out a dispirited monkey with a new one. Right away the new one went after the banana. The other monkeys attacked. The new monkey quickly learned to leave the banana alone, even though he didn't know why and had never been sprayed with cold water.

When a second new monkey was introduced to the group, the first new monkey joined the attack when the second new monkey made a move for the banana.

Eventually all the initial monkeys—the ones who had been blasted with cold water—were swapped out. Even so, none of the monkeys in the cage even tried for the banana.

Why not? Because the other monkeys beat them up, and *none of them knew why.*

Never let stupid monkeys tear you away from your dreams.

What was the problem when Joseph told his dream? Was it that his dream was too great, or that his brothers' dreams were too small? I'm glad he told his dream. And I'm glad he didn't wait for his brothers' approval to embrace his God-given vision of who he could become.

Although, I'm sure Joseph quickly regretted it. . . .

Law #4: God will never call you to violate your character, neglect your responsibilities, or exploit your relationships to fulfill your dreams.

Then his brothers went to feed their father's flock in Shechem. And Israel said to Joseph, "Are not your brothers feeding the flock in Shechem? Come, I will send you to them." So he said to him, "Here I am." Then he said to him, "Please go and see if it is well with your brothers and well with the flocks, and bring back word to me." So he sent him out of the Valley of Hebron, and he went to Shechem. Now a certain man found him, and there he was, wandering in the field. And the man asked him, saying, "What are you seeking?" So he said, "I am seeking my brothers. Please tell me where they are feeding their flocks." And the man said, "They have departed from here, for I heard them say, 'Let us go to Dothan.'" So Joseph went after his brothers and found them in Dothan.

Genesis 37:12–17

I remember the time I told my kids to pick up their junk from the floor and put it away. A few minutes later, I returned to see a half-done job.

"I told you guys to clean up your junk."

"We did clean up our junk," they said. "This stuff isn't junk. It's still good."

Kids are lawyers.

Most of us have our own Inner Lawyer on permanent retainer to justify our self-serving ways. This is what makes Joseph's actions stand out.

His father sent him to Shechem to prepare a performance review on the brothers. But Joseph discovered the brothers had relocated about twelve miles away, not in Shechem but in Dothan. His Inner Lawyer said, "Dad sent me to Shechem. I went to Shechem. They're not in Shechem. I'm done. Besides, I'm destined to rule and all this is beneath me."

But Joseph never permitted his Inner Lawyer to run his life. He rode twelve extra miles to Dothan to finish his father's assignment.

If he were my kid, I would have given him a coat of many colors too.

Menial labor wasn't beneath Joseph. He never let tomorrow's dreams make him neglect today's responsibilities.

God will never call you to violate your character, neglect your responsibilities, or exploit your relationships to fulfill your dreams.

43

This is one of the hardest laws to master. Joseph was destined to rule, yet he was out doing performance reviews on a gang of thugs called his brothers. Even in that, he went the extra mile. Character intact.

If you are going to reach your destiny God's way, you will not have to sin to do it. You will not have to renege on your promises, neglect your marriage, make your kids pay a price, or lie, cheat, or steal.

You won't have to shirk your responsibilities, breach a contract, or break your word.

You won't have to take time from your spouse or kids without their consent.

You have no thumbs-up from me to read this chapter, turn to your spouse, and say, "Honey, I'm cashing in junior's college fund to buy a surfboard because my destiny is to search the oceans for the perfect wave."

Your spouse might have something to say about that. Unless he or she is genuinely on board, you've missed God's dream for your life. When God calls you to a destiny, he calls your spouse too.

Another example: "Honey, I quit my day job because I'm gonna be a rock star!"

Right.

Jesus said, "Let your 'Yes' be 'Yes,' and your 'No,' 'No'" (Matthew 5:37).

When you said yes to a marriage, a family, a debt, or a contract, you gave your word to be a certain kind of person and to fulfill certain obligations. In God's mysterious ways, keeping your word on those obligations is the path to your dreams, even when it looks like it isn't.

If you won't go the extra mile where you're at today—with a good attitude—you won't develop the character it takes to sustain your dream-life tomorrow.

God-given dreams never look good on paper. God has to intervene or they won't happen. That's why it's essential you not manipulate people or events to bring them about. Leave room for the mysterious ways of God.

Character counts.

Keep your commitments. Stay faithful in little things. Go to Dothan. Then stand back and watch how God orchestrates the next steps in your life.

Just as he did for Joseph.

Law #5: You will reach your destiny only in ways that highlight the grace and glory of God.

Then they said to one another, "Look, this dreamer is coming! Come therefore, let us now kill him and cast him into some pit; and we shall say, 'Some wild beast has devoured him.' We shall see what will become of his dreams!"

Genesis 37:19–20

Are you sure you want your dream life?

Really sure?

The brothers called Joseph a new nickname: Dreamer. Actually, they called him "Lord of Dreams." Raise your hand if you'd like to play Thanksgiving football with brothers like that.

I'm sure an assassination conspiracy was not part of Joseph's master plan. Neither was being sold to slave traders heading toward Egypt. If this is what faithfulness gets you, who wants it, right?

Hold on to that question.

At this point, we have the bitter tale of brothers who washed their hands of Joseph and then covered up the whole affair. They killed a young goat and smeared blood on Joseph's coat of many colors—the symbol of their father's love. They brought it to Jacob, plastered innocent expressions on their lying faces, and said, "We can't find Joseph, but we found this bloody coat, and it looks like it might be his. What do you think, Dad?"

And he recognized it and said, "It is my son's tunic. A wild beast has devoured him. Without doubt Joseph is torn to pieces." Then Jacob tore his clothes, put sackcloth on his waist, and mourned for his son many days. And all his sons and all his daughters arose to comfort him; but he refused to be comforted, and he said, "For

45

I shall go down into the grave to my son in mourning." Thus his father wept for him. Now the Midianites had sold him in Egypt to Potiphar, an officer of Pharaoh and captain of the guard.

Genesis 37:33–36

Recently, a friend poured out his woes upon me. He was healthy, handsome, gainfully employed, and one of the youngest men I knew to buy his own home—a two-bedroom single-family home in super-expensive California. He told me how he had planned out every key detail of his life—his career, finances, and education. He planned when he would marry and when he'd start having kids. He produced written goals and a timeline. He had his life all planned out.

But life threw him some curve balls. My heart went out to him.

There he stood, sharing it all with me, sobbing because his girlfriend—the woman he was sure he would marry—just dumped him. That didn't figure into his destiny as he saw it. That wasn't his plan. He tortured himself, trying to figure out why God was being so cruel to him.

Immensely blessed, he faced one setback and was now bitter against God. Silly, right?

Don't rush to judgment.

When Moses wrote Joseph's story, he wanted you to ask some questions: Why can't God's path be easier? Why would God give Joseph a dream of greatness and then throw him into a pit and sell him into slavery? Why lift him to the heights of expectation only to dash him to the depths of disappointment?

Have you ever asked similar questions about your own life? Maybe God wove a beautiful tapestry for you on Monday and unraveled it on Tuesday. Why?

Perhaps God's Mr. McDreamy turned into Mr. McNightmare. Or you were sure God called you to start a business or invest in a company, but you've lost everything. Why?

Maybe the thing you prayed for came true, but now it tears your heart apart. What gives?

Jacob lost his favorite son, or so he thought. Why, God?

46

God destined Joseph for royalty, and then allowed him to be sold into slavery. How come? Why do troubles pile on? Where was God when Joseph groaned in the pit?

Before we can even attempt to answer such questions, we need to wrap our hearts around the fifth law of destiny: *You will reach your destiny only in ways that highlight the grace and glory of God.*

This truth is nicely summed up in two troubling Bible verses. Here's the first one:

> "For my thoughts are not your thoughts, nor are your ways my ways," says the LORD. "For as the heavens are higher than the earth, so are my ways higher than your ways, and my thoughts than your thoughts."
>
> Isaiah 55:8–9

In other words, it isn't for you to sit in judgment on the ways of God. He possesses the infinite wisdom of deity. By comparison, you and I boast the mental horsepower of a gnat. God, being omniscient, knows all the knowable. He has facts in evidence we have never considered.

God's thoughts won't fit in our mental box.

Never.

That's why your job is *faith*; God's job is *outcomes*. If you keep faith with God, heaven cheers you on, even if you fall flat on your face on earth.

God won't follow your preconceived map.

On your best days, you will acknowledge that as a good thing. This is why, when adversity strikes, Jeremiah Burroughs's definition becomes all-important: The deeply happy person "freely submits to and delights in God's wise and fatherly disposal in every condition."

You can never have a better, more gracious master than God. His ways are immeasurably better than yours. If you could see what God sees and feel what God feels, you would orchestrate your world exactly as God has orchestrated it, troubles included.

Oh yes, you would.

Once he plants the dream, the burden lies with him to make the way around the troubles.

There's no other reason I'm a preacher today. I planned against it. Like the old prophet Jonah, I hopped a ship the other way—I majored in anything but pastoral ministry. Yet here I am, fulfilling my destiny and experiencing my joy.

God planned it.

When I worked in a grocery store stacking apples, wondering how I would ever fulfill my dreams, God sent a man named Vern to call me—clear out of the blue—and offer a job in his church. Only God could have done that. Only God.

When I couldn't see how to finish school, a nearby Christian college launched the region's first-degree completion program, and its director was best friends with my pastor, so I got the news about it in time for the inaugural class. Only God.

When I ran out of money, God sent an unlikely friend to knock on my door and hand me a fat roll of money—twice—just to encourage me and keep me going. Only God.

When the ministry I was in felt too narrow for my dreams, a friend opened a basement for me to teach a Bible study, which grew into a new church, giving room to spread my wings. Only God.

God brought an introverted, embarrassed (though adorable) Italian son of a bartender into the ministry of the gospel. That eight-year-old boy with a sense of destiny looks back with a massive dose of wonder at a brilliant God who still makes dreams come true.

For Reflection and Discussion

1. Do you believe God still gives dreams or callings on a person's life? Why or why not?

2. If there were no obstacles, what dream would you pursue? Have you ever shared this with anyone? Why or why not?

3. What parts of your life seem to hold you back from pursuing your dreams?

4. How can you baby-step your way into your dreams, or at least a part of them? Is there a low-cost or low-impact way to do this?

5. What does Romans 8:32 tell you about God's heart toward you?

Secret
#3

Consistency

There is not an inch of any sphere of life of which Jesus
Christ the Lord does not say, "Mine."

—Abraham Kuyper

* * *

Spiritual Consistency

Be consistent with God, over time, in all the areas of life,
because your internal contradictions make you nuts.

* * *

One of These Things Just Doesn't Belong

In *The Godfather*, in one of the most intense scenes ever filmed,
Michael Corleone has presented his sister's infant son for chris-
tening, making Michael the Godfather. We watch as the child is
prepared and listen as the priest's haunting chant echoes through
the stone cathedral. The opening scene lifts you to a beautifully
spiritual plane.

As the camera pans across the cavernous space, Michael affirms his faith in the Triune God: the Father, the Son, and the Holy Spirit.

The camera zooms in on Michael as a priest asks the all-important question: "Do you renounce Satan?" The scene flashes to a man in a suit, hurrying down a hall. As you hear Michael say, "I do renounce Satan," you see the man draw a gun and blow away Michael's enemies. *Bang! Bang!* One dead body. *Bang!* Two dead bodies.

The killing is unnerving to watch. You've just been thrown off balance.

Scenes then alternate between the glorious church and murderous hit men raining vengeance on Michael's enemies. The priest asks, "And all his [Satan's] works?" Another gunshot. Three dead bodies.

"I do renounce them," says Michael. *Ratatatat!* A woman in bed, riddled with bullets from a Tommy gun. Four dead bodies.

"And all his pomp, and his promises?" the priest asks.

"I do renounce them." *Blam!* Three more dead bodies.

"Michael, will you be baptized?"

Answering on behalf of the child, he answers, "I will."

Church scene, murder scene. Church scene, murder scene. In rapid-fire succession. Chillingly brilliant, the viewer is forced to contemplate how any man can embrace such dramatic contradictions.

It's like the old *Sesame Street* Muppets' matching-and-sorting song about "one of these things" being not like the others. That's a skill you'll need for your spiritual life if you're going to live a happy life.

Disclaimer

Warning: Although the rest of this chapter is from the Bible, it's R-rated.

But before we dive into the racy stuff, I'd like to illustrate a little bit about how the Bible works.

In a smooth-running engine, the parts work together to make your car go. Odds are strong you wouldn't open your hood and randomly yank out parts just because you don't know what they do.

The stories of the Bible have been brilliantly *crafted* by their respective authors. Engineered, if you will. The parts work together to make the story go. Each part has a place. Unfortunately, many Bible readers, and even preachers, routinely yank out parts. That's because either we don't know what they do, or because we do know but disapprove.

Case in point: Genesis 38. The Joseph story flows smoothly from Genesis 37 through Genesis 50. The focus is clear. Like a master pyrotechnician, the author, Moses, arranges his fireworks in sequence, lights the fuses, and sets up a mind-blowing finale—so good it elicits "oohs" and "aahs" four thousand years after the fact.

We'll get there, soon.

All the parts work together. Good storytellers do that.

Genesis 38, however, seems to throw a raunchy bucket of ice water on Moses' well-planned fireworks.

A handful of scholars suggest the chapter doesn't belong in the story at all. They argue Genesis 38 is an "unconnected, independent, interruption . . . Every attentive reader can see that the story of Judah and Tamar has no connection at all with the strictly organized Joseph story." Another scholar alleges that this chapter "is like an alien element, suddenly and arbitrarily thrust into a record which it serves only to disturb. Certainly few people would choose this chapter as a basis for teaching or preaching."[1]

Let's prove that scholar wrong.

What if this chapter's shock to the system actually *serves* Joseph's storyline? What if it is the biblical author's "scared straight" approach to teaching about happiness?

As the World Turns

It's best if we stop right now to read Genesis 38 from the Bible. This is the story of Judah, Joseph's big brother. It's a rabbit-trail as far as Joseph's story goes, but its theme is right on. We'll bring it back to Joseph fast, I promise.

Final warning: The story is R-rated. Here you go.

About that time Judah left his brothers and went to stay with a man from Adullam whose name was Hirah. There Judah met the daughter of a Canaanite man whose name was Shua. He married her and slept with her. She became pregnant and gave birth to a son named Er. She became pregnant again and gave birth to another son, whom she named Onan. Then she became pregnant again and gave birth to another son, whom she named Shelah. He was born at Kezib.

Judah chose a wife for his firstborn son Er. Her name was Tamar. Er angered the Lord. So the Lord took away his life. Then Judah said to Onan, "Go sleep with your brother's widow. Do your duty for her as a brother-in-law, and produce a descendant for your brother." But Onan knew that the descendant wouldn't belong to him, so whenever he slept with his brother's widow, he wasted his semen on the ground to avoid giving his brother a descendant. What Onan did angered the Lord so much that the Lord took away Onan's life too.

Then Judah said to his daughter-in-law Tamar, "Return to your father's home. Live as a widow until my son Shelah grows up." He thought that this son, too, might die like his brothers. So Tamar went to live in her father's home.

After a long time Judah's wife, the daughter of Shua, died. When Judah had finished mourning, he and his friend Hirah from Adullam went to Timnah where the men were shearing Judah's sheep. As soon as Tamar was told that her father-in-law was on his way to Timnah to shear his sheep, she took off her widow's clothes, covered her face with a veil, and disguised herself. Then she sat down at the entrance to Enaim, which is on the road to Timnah. (She did this because she realized that Shelah was grown up now, and she hadn't been given to him in marriage.)

When Judah saw her, he thought she was a prostitute because she had covered her face. Since he didn't know she was his daughter-in-law, he approached her by the roadside and said, "Come on, let's sleep together!"

She asked, "What will you pay to sleep with me?"

"I'll send you a young goat from the flock," he answered.

She said, "First give me something as a deposit until you send it."

"What should I give you as a deposit?" he asked.

"Your signet ring, its cord, and the shepherd's staff that's in your hand," she answered.

So he gave them to her. Then he slept with her, and she became pregnant. After she got up and left, she took off her veil and put her widow's clothes back on.

Judah sent his friend Hirah to deliver the young goat so that he could get back his deposit from the woman, but his friend couldn't find her. He asked the men of that area, "Where's that prostitute who was beside the road at Enaim?"

"There's no prostitute here," they answered.

So he went back to Judah and said, "I couldn't find her. Even the men of that area said, 'There's no prostitute here.'"

Then Judah said, "Let her keep what I gave her, or we'll become a laughingstock. After all, I did send her this young goat, but you couldn't find her."

About three months later Judah was told, "Your daughter-in-law Tamar has been acting like a prostitute. What's more, because of it she's pregnant."

Judah ordered, "Bring her out to be burned."

As she was brought out, she sent a message to her father-in-law, "I'm pregnant by the man who owns these things. See if you recognize whose signet ring, cord, and shepherd's staff these are."

Judah recognized them and said, "She's not guilty. I am! She did this because I haven't given her my son Shelah." Judah never made love to her again.

The time came for Tamar to give birth, and she had twin boys. When she was giving birth, one of them put out his hand. The midwife took a piece of red yarn, tied it on his wrist, and said, "This one came out first." As he pulled back his hand, his brother was born. So she said, "Is this how you burst into the world!" He was named Perez [Bursting Into]. After that his brother was born with the red yarn on his hand. He was named Zerah [Sunrise].

Genesis 38 (GW)

Quite a soap opera, isn't it? Let's review. While little brother Joseph was getting dragged off to Egypt, the spotlight shifted to his older brother Judah. You might think Judah would set a sterling example of contentment and love for God, being a big brother and all.

Think again.

The problems started when Judah married a woman from the morally depraved, idol-worshiping culture of the Canaanites—thus thumbing his nose at both his grandfather's and his great-grandfather's unmistakable instructions (Genesis 28:1; 24:3).[2]

They bore three sons as pleasant as an untweezed hair.

Judah's firstborn, Er, married a woman named Tamar, and died from a terminal case of wickedness (Genesis 38:7). The spotlight turned to his widow, Tamar.

In those days a widow was vulnerable. She had little means of income. Seen as a financial liability, she had severed her limb from her own family tree and been grafted onto her husband's family tree. But when her husband died, the widow had nothing, unless her rights were maintained *by her father-in-law,* in this case, Judah. For Tamar, those rights included an heir of the rich bloodline of Judah.

Knowing this, Judah instructed his second son to take Tamar as a wife and produce an heir for his brother.

The conversation went like this:

JUDAH: "Hey, Onan, what are you doing?"

ONAN: "Just oiling the blades on our sheep-shearing knives."

JUDAH: "Oh, great. I have another job for you. Now that your brother is dead, I need you to marry Tamar and get her pregnant. As you know, legally the first son won't belong to you. Legally, he'll replace your dead brother, Er."

ONAN: "Errr . . ."

Onan was smart enough to do the math. Dad had three sons and a boatload of money—not to mention the lucrative inheritance going back three generations to Abraham. There was a lot of money at stake.

Under their system, the oldest son received a double portion of the inheritance. So *before* Er died, Judah's lucrative inheritance would be split up this way:

Er: 50 percent

Onan: 25 percent

Shelah: 25 percent

But now that Er is dead, guess who was oldest and in line for the double portion?

Onan: 66 percent

Shelah: 33 percent

So Onan understood if he raised up an heir for Er—let's call him Ernie—Ernie stood in succession as Er himself. Ernie, therefore, would get the firstborn's inheritance, dropping Onan from a lofty 66 percent right back down to paltry 25 percent.

What's a little brother to do? Onan married Tamar but adopted the withdrawal method of birth control. "Sorry, Tamar—no baby for you." In this twisted tale, what do you call that? *A death sentence.* God took Onan out of the picture too—permanently.

Let's pause the story for a question about a happy life: Who in this story lays a happy head upon their pillow at night? So far, nobody. Two dead sons, one grieving father, and one twice-over widow that nobody is willing to help.

Let's dig deeper: Why was Judah such a spiritual bonehead? Why was he hanging with Canaanite friends? Why did he marry a Canaanite woman? And what kind of father was he that his sons go down in the history books for their wickedness? Judah's family tree dripped more drama than a teenager's phone calls, even though he descended from a lineage of faith's champions (Hebrews 11:17–21). Where did Judah go wrong?

Can anyone really pray for a God-blessed life while simultaneously embracing a godless lifestyle?

Can you be spiritually inconsistent and spiritually satisfied at the same time?

Can you pray on Sunday and sleep with a prostitute on Monday and call it good?

Can you renounce Satan even as you blast your enemies to kingdom come?

Back to the story.

Gotta Do What You Gotta Do

Having now lost two sons, Judah was understandably jittery about marrying off son #3 to Tamar. He stalled. He stalled some more. Meanwhile, back at her father's ranch, Tamar's biological clock was tick-tick-ticking.

Finally, enough was enough. Tamar hatched a plan. Dressing as a prostitute—actually, the Hebrew original indicates a temple prostitute—she tricked Judah himself—yes, her own father-in-law—into a sexual fling. She knew right where to wait for him and exactly when he'd get off work.

Tired from sheep-shearing and ready for Miller Time, Judah spotted a "nameless" veiled prostitute, settled a price, and did the deed.

Tamar got pregnant.

Papa Judah didn't have a clue he had just had sex with his daughter-in-law or that he'd gotten her pregnant.

Around baby-bump time, Judah heard about the pregnancy.

"Aha!" he said to himself. "She's an adulterer!" A perfect end to a long-term problem. Judah called for Tamar's death. "Burn her!" he shouted. "Bad, bad person for having sex outside of marriage!"

Consistency issues?

The executioners gathered, but at the very moment she was to be put to death, Tamar whipped out the calling card of the guy who got her pregnant.

"Excuse me, sir. The man who did this to me gave me this. Perhaps you can find him and burn him too, right?"

A flush of red spread from Judah's cheeks to his ears as he recognized his signet, cord, and staff. He gulped air and hung his head. Speechless, the events of that nine-months-ago one-night stand raced through his mind like a bad dream. It all made horrible sense. The sheep shearing. The woman dressed as a temple prostitute. Justice denied for a vulnerable woman. She had planned it all.

Through a thick throat, he acknowledged his transgression: "Put down your torches. She's not guilty. I am."

And they all lived miserably ever after.

Frankenstein's Monster

What can Judah's long-ago and far-away story possibly say to our lives today? And what does it have to do with creating a happy life?

Let's think "Frankenstein's monster" for a moment. How did Dr. Frankenstein make him? He stitched together body parts from lots of different sources. That's what made him creepy.

Judah's life was like that. He stitched together a lot of parts that shouldn't go together. One day he was an exalted heir of the promises of God. The next day he was a spiritual moron. His best friend was an idol-worshiping Canaanite (think *Nazi*), who was nothing but a bad influence. He disrespected the women in his life. He disrespected the laws of God. He married outside his faith. He raised evil sons. He slept with a prostitute yet wanted to execute his daughter-in-law for adultery.

His life had become an irreconcilable assemblage of contradictory parts.

Like Michael Corleone, his values on Monday contradicted his choices on Tuesday. What he prayed for on Wednesday he sabotaged on Thursday. His commitments on Friday he broke on Saturday. And then on Sunday he dragged himself to church wondering why he was so frustrated and why God kept letting him down.

Some advice: Be consistent with God, over time, in all areas of life, because your internal contradictions make you nuts.

You cannot compartmentalize your spirituality from the rest of your life and expect to be happy.

You have to let God and his truth flow into your financial life, your married or dating life, your parenting, your work life, your career, your sex life, your retirement, your words, your thoughts, and your actions. Give him an all-access pass to your life and your drama—or risk the crackpot emotions of trying to contain in one soul both matter and antimatter.

> But let him ask in faith, without wavering; for he who wavers is like a surge of the sea, wind-driven and tossed. Such a man need not suppose that he will receive anything from the Lord, double-minded as he is, unstable at every turn.
>
> James 1:6–8 MNT[3]

When you pray "Dear God, help me lose weight" while standing in the grocery line with a mega-pack of Oreos in one hand and a super-sized Ben and Jerry's in the other, you have become James's double-minded person. Your prayer goes no higher than the ceiling—not because God has turned his back on you, but because your choices unravel your prayers as fast as you knit them. You are living an absurdity, incarnating a contradiction.

You sabotage your own happiness. Like Barney Fife, you shoot yourself in the foot.

When Judah married a Canaanite, he did something unrighteous. When he offered his second son to Tamar, he did something righteous. When he committed adultery with Tamar, he did something unrighteous—especially so, since she was dressed as a Canaanite temple prostitute, i.e., a pagan religion the Jews were supposed to keep a million miles away from. When he demanded her burning, he wore his sanctimonious anti-adultery hat.

Like a six-year-old boy of health-conscious parents unleashed in a candy store for the first time—grasping like a maniac in every direction—Judah grasped anything that might conceivably offer the hint of even the most fleeting spasm of happiness. Even when the choices were self-contradictory.

Like Michael Corleone, he introduced internal conflicts his soul couldn't bear.

These kinds of inconsistencies will destroy our joy. They fracture our contentment because they fracture our souls. They make us crazy.

Not to get too ahead of the story, but the main character, Joseph, in the space of only two chapters, will honor God's authority not only in his spiritual life, but in his work life and sexual life too.

He was consistent with God across all the areas of his life.

Company's Coming

Imagine inviting Jesus to your place for dinner. In preparation, you clean the bathroom, prepare the meal, and set the table. You throw the dirty laundry into the bedroom and shut the door. You hide the clutter from the counter, cramming it inside the junk drawer, and then shove your few magazines—the latest copy of *People*, the new *Globe,* and the stack of *Cosmos*—into the coffee table drawer. You even erase your online browsing history.

Finally, Jesus arrives. Hugs and laughter all around.

Once inside, to your horror, he heads straight for the bedroom. Jesus throws open the door and reveals the giant mound of dirty laundry. A flush creeps across your face. He reaches under the nightstand and pulls out that racy novel with the mostly naked couple on the cover. You examine your feet, wondering where that gaping chasm is when you need one. When he gets to your computer, he reaches into his back pocket, smiles, and pulls out a printout of all the sites you've visited. "Surprise!" he says. You cough and wipe the sweat from your brow.

"J-Jesus," you stutter, "I thought we were just having dinner. What are you doing?"

"Oh," he says. "I like to do a deep-cleaning first—it makes dinner taste so much better." He smiles. "Don't worry—it's *gratis.* The bill's on me."

Groan.

Jesus doesn't play by anybody's rules but his own. He won't stay put. You can't squeeze him into the living room and shut him out from the bedroom. Once he's in, he's in. He'll poke around everywhere, like it or not.

Why would Jesus do that?

Because he loves you enough to deliver you from the mortal enemy of your happiness.

Pleonexia: The Frantic Search for Happiness

Desperate people do crazy things. Have you ever done something stupid and wondered, *Where did that come from?* Biblically, it comes from a conflicted soul. The Bible describes it like this:

> Having their understanding darkened, being alienated from the life of God, because of the ignorance that is in them, because of the blindness of their heart; who, being past feeling, have given themselves over to lewdness, to work all uncleanness with greediness.
>
> Ephesians 4:18–19

Every line of that statement describes the inner life of Judah. We're going to see very soon that it also describes the *exact opposite* of Joseph's inner life.

The last word, *greediness,* translates the New Testament Greek word *pleonexia* (pronounced *play-oh-nex-EEE-ah*). Pleonexia has a depth of meaning no single word can capture. One translation puts it, "A continual lust for more."[4] Plato discussed it. The Greeks philosophized over it. And Christians dissected it. An ancient Latin writer called it "the accursed love of possessing."[5]

An early church pastor defined it as "the aiming always at getting more, the snatching of things which it does not befit a man to have."[6]

A person with a case of pleonexia has one simple motto: "More."

One scholar outlined five variations on the pleonexia theme in the New Testament. Here they are in modified form. I'm including the relevant Bible verses so you can do more study on your own.

1. A person who practices the opposite of God's generosity and love; a person who kicks Christian charity to the curb (Romans 1:29–30).

2. A person who evaluates life in material terms (Luke 12:15).
3. A person who builds himself up at the expense of others; an exploiter (1 Thessalonians 2:5; 2 Peter 2:3).
4. A person who worships things instead of God (Colossians 3:5).
5. A person who indulges sexual sin in a frantic search for happiness (Mark 7:22 and Ephesians 4:19).[7]

Don't rush past this. Pause and consider your heart. Contemplate your ways.

Have you bought in to any part of the pleonexia lie?

Judah, Onan, and their friends are poster children for pleonexia. Pleonexia manifests as a frantic search for happiness. Once you're bitten by this bug, you'll find no deep happiness at all—not in God, not in family, not in possessions, not in anything. You can't be satisfied, because you'll never have enough. It's impossible because of the condition of your own soul.

What makes this even more difficult is the delusion that you *can* have enough, *if only* . . .

- If only you can tease a sexy smile from your neighbor's spouse, or
- If only you can have sparkly jewelry like your best friend's, or
- If only you can ink a deal to match your co-worker's salary, or
- If only you can afford your gym buddy's plastic surgery, or
- If only you can be as popular as the prom king or queen, or
- If only you can win the lottery.

Pleonexia seduces you into one more drink, one more roll of the dice, one more rendezvous with a forbidden love, one more juicy gossip session, one more click of the mouse, one more size on the implants—and *then* you'll be happy.

But you won't be happy, because the thing you're grasping for can't make you happy. You may get what you want—like Judah— but you won't want what you get—like Judah.

Pleonexia over-promises and under-delivers every time.

That disappointment stokes the fires of your search even more, trapping you in the moral whirlpool of Ephesians 4:17–19.

Even worse, pleonexia cross-contaminates all the compartments of your life. Dishonest dealings in the financial department will manifest as dissatisfaction in the sexual compartment. Unfaithfulness in the marriage compartment can show up as frustration in the career compartment. And all of this makes you snap at the kids in the parenting compartment.

The simple fact of life is that your soul has no compartments; no airtight bulkheads exist to prevent the pleonexia cockroach from infesting every corner of your heart.

Your deep happiness is not a function of what you have or don't have; it's a matter of uniting your soul under the influence of God.

Get It Together

Truth is reality.

Truth is reality as God experiences it, God defines it, and God reveals it.

You can't break God's truth; you can only break yourself against God's truth.

Insanity embraces unreality as a toddler embraces a teddy bear against the night's terrors. When you base any corner of your life on unreality, you fracture your soul and happiness leaks out. You pound yourself against the bedrock truth of God and wonder why life is so frustrating.

Stop it.

The sleazy tale of Onan, Judah, and Tamar is here on purpose. It is a divinely inspired reality check on our journey toward happiness. One road leads to wholeness. The other to brokenness and fragmentation.

Which road will you choose?

Ever feel like you're cracking up? Scatterbrained? Falling apart? Going to pieces? Even our language reflects society's awareness of a fragmented soul.

God invites you to a better way. You can pray:

> Teach me your way, O LORD; I will walk in your truth;
> Unite my heart to fear your name.
>
> Psalm 86:11

Maybe it's time to ask God's help to get all the voices in your head singing the same tune. *Unite my heart, God. Bring together all my faculties to respect you all the days of my life. Let all the parts of me honor you in each and every moment of each and every day.*

Michael Corleone died old and alone—a broken, damaged man, full of regrets. He embraced contradictions his soul couldn't bear.

Judah staged a minor spiritual comeback; we'll see that in his future dealings with Joseph.

Tamar did pretty well, becoming an unlikely ancestor of Jesus. When the Bible says Jesus was born from the tribe of Judah, you get the idea that God accomplishes his cosmic purposes even through royally messed-up people.

I feel safe with a God who can do that. Safe enough to willingly open all the doors of my inner mansion to him.

What about you? Consistency or fragmentation? Happiness or pleonexia? Your call.

FOR REFLECTION AND DISCUSSION

1. Have you ever been shocked to discover that a certain person claimed to be a Christian? What inconsistencies did you notice?

2. In what ways might the story be different if Onan had fulfilled his obligation? Are there any obligations you're reluctant to fulfill?

3. Are there any ways your choices are contradicting your prayers these days? What changes might you need to make?

4. How has the frantic search for happiness played out in your life?

5. Have you observed people who were once on fire for God but now show no discernible link with him? What can turn a person off like that?

6. What does Jesus teach about consistency in Matthew 6:24?

Secret
#**4**

Loyalty

I would like to buy three dollars worth of God, please. Not enough to explode my soul or disturb my sleep, but just enough to equal a cup of warm milk or a snooze in the sunshine. I don't want enough of him to make me love a black man or pick beets with a migrant. I want ecstasy, not transformation; I want the warmth of the womb, not a new birth. I want a pound of the Eternal in a paper sack. I would like to buy three dollars worth of God, please.[1]

—Wilbur Reese

* * *

Unwavering Loyalty

Reciprocate the immeasurable loyalty of God to you by your own loyalty back to him, because moral shortcuts make happiness fizzle.

* * *

Hachiko

Buck, John Thornton's dog in *The Call of the Wild*, has stiff competition for the blue ribbon in the loyalty category.

At a train station in Japan, riders are greeted by a bronze statue of an Akita—a large breed of dog from Japan's northern regions. The statue memorializes Hachiko, truest super-dog.

His master, Professor Ueno, lived in Tokyo and commuted to work daily from the train station. Every day, Hachiko escorted his master to the station in the morning and returned every evening for a slobbery greeting and a happy walk home.

One day in May 1925, Professor Ueno suffered a fatal heart attack while at work.

Hachiko waited patiently at the station, but would never see his master again.

The loyal dog was given to new owners. Nothing could stop him, however, from scouring the city for his master. Hachiko even found his old home and made the heartbreaking discovery that his master didn't live there anymore.

He searched the train station. He wouldn't give up.

Every day, Hachiko waited at the exact time Professor Ueno's train was scheduled to arrive. Every day, alert eyes searched the deboarding passengers. Every day, a growing family of friends fed the dog, petted him, and showered him with affection. Hachiko wormed his way into their hearts, a living monument to unwavering loyalty.

Every day, slumped ears slinked home to new masters, who, though loving, could never replace the professor.

Hachiko returned to the station every day for eleven years.

He inspired a nation. Schoolteachers told his story to instill dedication in children. Parents reminded their kids of the persistent loyalty of Hachiko.

In 1934, a statue was placed in his spot; the loyal animal was there for the festivities. A year later, Hachiko died. He never gave up his doggy-dream of once again licking his master's face.

A Stressed-Out Poodle?

When we last saw Joseph, his sweet, caring, gentle big brothers had knocked him on the head, thrown him into a pit, and sat down for lunch while Joseph cried out for rescue. Later that day, they sold him to slave traders headed toward Egypt.

A captain in the Egyptian army, named Potiphar, bought him.

And so our hero, the royal dreamer, found himself a slave in an Egyptian household, a universe away from a home he would never see again.

The only person who might think of rescuing him—his father, Jacob—has already mourned his death.

If anybody has ever had a right to complain, it was Joseph. He *should* feel sorry for himself. His family let him down. His brothers betrayed him. The world splattered him with spitballs. If I were Joseph, I would back into a corner and lick my wounds like a stressed-out poodle.

But Joseph rose above both his dysfunctional family and his depressing predicament. He stayed loyal to the One who stayed loyal to him.

Lie With Me

Genesis 39 offers a soap opera in four scenes. Let's think through the second one first; you'll see why in a moment.

> And it came to pass after these things that his master's wife cast longing eyes on Joseph, and she said, "Lie with me." But he refused and said to his master's wife, "Look, my master does not know what is with me in the house, and he has committed all that he has to my hand. There is no one greater in this house than I, nor has he kept back anything from me but you, because you are his wife. How then can I do this great wickedness, and sin against God?" So it was, as she spoke to Joseph day by day, that he did not heed her, to lie with her or to be with her. But it happened about this time, when Joseph went into the house to do his work, and none of the men of the house was inside, that she caught him by his garment, saying, "Lie with me." But he left his garment in her hand, and fled and ran outside.
>
> Genesis 39:7–12

Joseph: strong and handsome, a desirable young man in the prime of life.

Mrs. Potiphar: lonely, desperate, and used to getting what she wants.

A perfect recipe for a satisfying evening of deeply meaningful sex, don't you think? What's a young guy to do? His father's house and his family's faith are distant memories. Nobody would know. Any virile young man would do it. His older brother (Judah) wouldn't give it a moment's thought—we saw that a chapter ago.

What are the odds a young man with a dysfunctional past would turn down a rich, hot, aggressive cougar?

Joseph said no. He defied the odds; reined in his hormones. "How can I do this great wickedness and sin against God?" he asked.

Coming, as it does, on the heels of Judah's whoremongering and Onan's egocentrism, Joseph's fidelity shines like a diamond in a dung heap.

Joseph remained loyal to his boss, Potiphar. Potiphar entrusted everything to Joseph: the house, the grounds, the other servants, his businesses, his checkbook, his social security number, all the passwords for his online accounts. Potiphar has not kept back even one thing from Joseph's authority, he said.

Except Mrs. Potiphar.

Now every day she grabbed him and begged/commanded/cajoled him to have sex with her.

What are the odds?

Joseph remained loyal to Potiphar because he remained loyal to God.

Your sexual life is a matter of loyalty to God.

That's important.

When your loyalty to God is bigger than your loyalty to your peer group or your girlfriend or your boyfriend or your neighbor's spouse—when your loyalty to God rises head and shoulders above every other loyalty—that's when you'll begin to find the happiness God designed you for.

But loyalty to God reaches into every area of life, not just sexuality. It touches your relationships, dating, marriage, finances, parenting, career choice, mission, purpose, fitness—everything.

You may have your own Mrs. Potiphar tugging your sleeve right now, begging to you to hop into bed with her. Money, materialism, sex, greed, power, drugs, alcoholism, cheating, theft, despair. Who's your Mrs. Potiphar?

You swim in a sea of monsters competing for your allegiance. Without an unwavering loyalty to God, you will be devoured. You will be drawn away from the single force in the universe that brings lasting satisfaction.

You have to say no.

Actually, you need to do more than that.

You need to run away fast, because that way God will reward you big-time, right?

Not so fast.

> And so it was, when she saw that he had left his garment in her hand and fled outside, that she called to the men of her house and spoke to them, saying, "See, he has brought in to us a Hebrew to mock us. He came in to me to lie with me, and I cried out with a loud voice. And it happened, when he heard that I lifted my voice and cried out, that he left his garment with me, and fled and went outside." So she kept his garment with her until his master came home. Then she spoke to him with words like these, saying, "The Hebrew servant whom you brought to us came in to me to mock me; so it happened, as I lifted my voice and cried out, that he left his garment with me and fled outside." So it was, when his master heard the words which his wife spoke to him, saying, "Your servant did to me after this manner," that his anger was aroused. Then Joseph's master took him and put him into the prison, a place where the king's prisoners were confined. And he was there in the prison.
>
> Genesis 39:13–20

Mrs. Potiphar sure was a sweetheart. I'll bet she baked cookies for all the boys and girls on holidays. Joseph was a picture of loyalty. Mrs. Potiphar was a picture of back-stabbing treachery.

Hell hath no fury like Mrs. Potiphar scorned. She accused Joseph of attempted sexual assault. She blamed her husband for bringing Joseph into the house to begin with. She used the coat she had grabbed off him as evidence against him. She stood by as Joseph was thrown into prison.

I'd love to see the look on her face in that moment. Disloyal to God, her husband, Joseph, and the truth. She's a peach. Don't miss the contrasts:

- Joseph was a slave; Mrs. Potiphar was a high-ranking official's wife.
- Joseph was poor; Mrs. P. was loaded.
- Joseph was in a foreign land; Mrs. P. was in her homeland.
- Joseph had no power and no rights; Mrs. P. had all the power and all the rights.
- Joseph was all alone; Mrs. P. was surrounded by a husband, a marriage, friends, family, and servants.
- Joseph had no properties; Mrs. P. had a lavish estate.
- Joseph had nothing; Mrs. P. had everything.

So who's happy? Who's living a deeply satisfied life?

Sooner or later we have to knit our emotions to the fabric of truth: *Happiness does not depend on the quality of your stuff; it depends on the condition of your heart.* If your heart is right with God, you have all the ingredients you need for a truly happy life. Even if you're stuck in a faraway land. Even if the boss's spouse is hitting on you. Even if the insanity virus makes your family tree a hot zone. Even if anything.

I have to confess how much I dislike this truth. As much as I preach it and try to live it, the strong muscles in my knuckles lock tightly on my goods and refuse to let go. I'm a pastor—a preacher of the oracles of God, for crying out loud. I shouldn't be this materialistic.

If there is any comfort to be found in God's call to flee whatever Mrs. Potiphars would drag me to beds of death, it is this: God has something better in store for me.

To push this deeper, let's notice that Moses serves up an important morsel in verse 8: Not only did Joseph "refuse" Mrs. Potiphar's advances, he did so repeatedly, stubbornly, and over a sustained period.[2]

Like Hachiko.

Loyalty that doesn't last isn't loyalty.

It's a spasm.

Just Whose Loyalty Counts Most?

Confession time: I'm playing a sort of trick on you by setting Joseph's loyalty in the spotlight. Yes, it's important, but it's not most important.

What's most important is someone else's loyalty—a detail routinely overlooked in this place in the Bible. Let me wave my biblical wand and bring out a deeper truth in the text.

It's time to back up to the first paragraph. Read it with this question in mind: *What good deed does Joseph do in this paragraph?*

Now Joseph had been taken down to Egypt. And Potiphar, an officer of Pharaoh, captain of the guard, an Egyptian, bought him from the Ishmaelites who had taken him down there. The LORD was with Joseph, and he was a successful man; and he was in the house of his master the Egyptian. And his master saw that the LORD was with him and that the LORD made all he did to prosper in his hand. So Joseph found favor in his sight, and served him. Then he made him overseer of his house, and all that he had he put under his authority. So it was, from the time that he had made him overseer of his house and all that he had, that the LORD blessed the Egyptian's house for Joseph's sake; and the blessing of the LORD was on all that he had in the house and in the field. Thus he left all that he had in Joseph's hand, and he did not know what he had except for the bread which he ate. Now Joseph was handsome in form and appearance.

Genesis 39:1–6

Look carefully. Joseph does no good deed whatsoever in this paragraph. He is not portrayed as faithful. He is not portrayed as loyal. He is not portrayed as good. He is not portrayed as anything except the recipient of Somebody Else's loyalty.

Whose?

- The Lord was with Joseph and he was a successful man (v. 2).
- His master saw that the Lord was with him (v. 3).
- The Lord made all he did to prosper (v. 3).
- The Lord blessed the Egyptian's house for Joseph's sake (v. 5).
- The blessing of the Lord was on all that he had (v. 5).
- Joseph was handsome "in form and in appearance" (v. 6). Who gets credit for that?

Whose loyalty does Scripture spotlight?

God stuck to Joseph like Hachiko stuck to Professor Ueno. God was there for him; God orchestrated the best possible outcomes even within the worst possible context.

God is infinitely more committed to us than we will ever be to him. Let that sink in.

A little more. Let it sink down to your toes.

The core truth of the Christian faith is not your morality, duty, obedience, good works, or anything you might do for God. It is the epic adventure of God-became-man and what he has done—and will do—for you. In the Christian story, God does the work, God pays the price, God proves his love again and again.

God is the supremely loyal one.

One of the occupational hazards of growing up Christian is the relentless exposure to behavioral messages. The first two decades of my life were spent running around a church, serving God.

I was so busy being loyal to him that I forgot he was far more loyal to me.

That morphed into the lunacy that my loyalty to him actually triggered his loyalty to me, as if God were waiting for me to be good to him, and then he would grudgingly send a little goodness back my way.

Listen to a hundred sermons, read a hundred books from the Christian shelves . . . my hunch is that the overwhelming message is we should do more for God. Radical love. Crazy commitment. Unwavering loyalty. All are good messages.

But all are futile messages unless the loyalty, love, and commitment are clearly seen to emanate from God first and are only then reciprocated by us. Most of us have it backward.

"We love him because he first loved us," (1 John 4:19) said John. We need to remember the "he first loves us" part every single day.

Underline *first*.

My faith wore me down because I had it backward.

My loyalty wasn't a reciprocation of his loyalty; his was a reciprocation of mine, or so I thought.

Over time, I've come to see it is not my loyalty to God that counts most but his loyalty to me. The grand story of Scripture is the epic of a God who made me, watched me run from him as fast as my depraved legs could carry me, and bought me back to himself at unspeakable cost. The Bible is, above all else, the story of God's loyalty.

God is infinitely more loyal to me than I will ever be to him.

To whatever degree that mind-blowing revelation is woven into the fabric of my thinking and believing, I will reciprocate with gratitude-induced loyalty back to him.

Plus, I'll be normal, the way God intended. Not weird.

And happy.

Loyalty Goes to Jail

As you read the final paragraph in Genesis 39, once again, look at whose loyalty takes center stage.

> Then Joseph's master took him and put him into the prison, a place where the king's prisoners were confined. And he was there in the prison. But the LORD was with Joseph and showed

him mercy, and he gave him favor in the sight of the keeper of the prison. And the keeper of the prison committed to Joseph's hand all the prisoners who were in the prison; whatever they did there, it was his doing. The keeper of the prison did not look into anything that was under Joseph's authority, because the LORD was with him; and whatever he did, the LORD made it prosper.

Genesis 39:20–23

Did you catch the emphasis?

- The Lord was with Joseph (v. 21).
- The Lord showed him mercy (v. 21).
- The Lord gave him favor in the warden's eyes (vv. 21–22).
- The Lord was with him (v. 23).
- Whatever Joseph did, the Lord made it prosper (v. 23).

The Scripture here does not direct us to look at any quality in Joseph at all. It sets up flashing neon pointers to the unwavering loyalty of God.

Cast-iron prison bars cannot block the loyalty of God.

Corrupt bankers cannot block the loyalty of God.

Whacked-out politicians cannot block the loyalty of God.

Shadowy conspirators cannot block the loyalty of God.

Crazy siblings cannot block the loyalty of God.

Unjust judges cannot block the loyalty of God.

Crooked lawyers cannot block the loyalty of God.

Culture gone wild cannot block the loyalty of God.

By my count this story contains at least a dozen explicit statements of God's loyalty to Joseph. There is only one explicit statement of Joseph's loyalty to God (v. 9).

God wins.

When Potiphar's wife grabbed Joseph's sleeve to drag him to bed, Joseph responded with monumental loyalty to God. But that loyalty didn't emerge from a vacuum. It was the by-product of a deeply rooted confidence in the unwavering loyalty of God—a confidence we can hold even when our world caves in. You can rest your frantic soul, content in the love of a God whose loyalty reaches to the skies.

So What?

1. Just because you're on the downhill slide, it doesn't mean that God has forsaken you.

Joseph's mother died. His brothers hated him. They stripped him naked and dumped him unceremoniously into slavery. He lost his father's love.

But the Lord was with Joseph, and that made all the difference.

When everything goes wrong, you can still be confident that God is with you. He's got your back.

Joseph never kicks faith to the curb. He clamps a viselike grip on the royal dream and on the God who gave it, and never lets go. More important, he looks up to see a good God who has clamped a viselike grip on him, and Joseph realizes that just because things are hard for him, it doesn't mean they are hard for God.

A truly happy soul feels the grip of God, no matter how fast the downhill slide may be.

2. The more you are convinced of the love of God, the more you can reciprocate with your love for God.

Joseph's story establishes the loyalty of God before it ever moves on to the loyalty of Joseph. Keep it in that order, okay?

Christians swing to two equal and opposite errors with regard to the love of God. They either underestimate his love and feel they've got to earn it, or they overestimate their worthiness and transmogrify God's love into something mushy and meaningless—as if every kid deserves a trophy.

Neither is true.

You don't have to earn it, but it does have to be earned, and you're not worthy. Only Christ could earn it, and he did. His death and resurrection opened the floodgates of infinite love. All of God's love flows to us at great expense; there's nothing mushy or meaningless about it.

And there's nothing in us to make us worthy.

Sorry.

If you try to love God but doubt his love, you'll get trapped in a gigantic hamster wheel of performance. You'll never feel the love of God because you're too busy trying to earn it.

God comes to you and says, "I never loved you because of who and what you are, but only because of who and what I am. Even with your failures, I still love you."

That little anxiety in your spirit that makes you feel like you have to prove yourself worthy—that anxiety is the kiss of death to happiness.

3. "God has provided everything I need for my present happiness."

I like this definition of contentment I first heard as a kid: *Contentment means believing God has provided everything I need for my present happiness.*

Do you believe that? Is God actually that loyal? Or is this just spiritual mumbo-jumbo designed to psych you into a phony religious happy place?

Scripture writes across the starry sky the story of a faithful God. His heart imagined the beauties of our world, and his hand brought them forth. His love conspired with his righteousness to create the gracious plan of salvation. By that plan, he reconciles fallen humans to himself. In that plan, he makes peace with God not only possible but actual.

God then implemented that plan through the shed blood of his Son.

If God would go that far to save you, why wouldn't he do the dramatically easier thing of taking care of you?

He who did not spare his own Son, but delivered him up for us all, how shall he not with him also freely give us all things?

Romans 8:32

By "all things" God means gas in your car when you need it, bread in your pantry when you need it, open arms for an embrace when you need it, cash in your bank account when you need it, a word of encouragement when you need it, and a gut-busting belly laugh when you need it.

Your sudden need did not startle God from a nice snooze. He saw it coming long ago. From eternity past, God looked forward down the corridors of time. He saw every need you would ever face. He foresaw every opportunity and every adversity. He knew your pleasures and your pains before you lived them. He heard every prayer you would pray. He even knew the prayers you should have prayed but didn't.

God not only knew these things, he made absolutely perfect provision for every single one of them.

Whatever you need, you have it right on time. He is not early and he is not late. God promised to "supply all your need according to his riches in glory by Christ Jesus" (Philippians 4:19).

God has provided everything you need for your present happiness.

You might object, "Hey, I really needed [insert need here] and God didn't supply it! What gives?"

Most likely you confused a *want* with a *need*. The fact that you're still around to read this book proves you really didn't *need* [insert supposed need here].

Plus, as we'll see later, what looks like a gap in God's provision just might be God setting you up for something bigger and better down the road.

Our problem is not a lack of provision.

It's a lack of confidence.

Your God is too small.

Through faith, St. Paul could say he had learned to be content no matter what state he was in (Philippians 4:11).

Every page of Scripture sings the praise of a great God who shows up big when we need him.

Joseph proves God can deliver happiness across borders and behind locked doors.

Joseph could be happy and not sleep with another man's wife. He could be happy and not hate his brothers. He could be happy and not resent God for the twists and turns of fate.

For Joseph, the loyalty of God was enough. With that, he could lay a contented head on his pillow every night, in a land a lifetime away from his dreams.

His hands may have been empty but his heart was full.

It can be that way for you.

FOR REFLECTION AND DISCUSSION

1. Has a life of faith seemed like a chore to you? An endless to-do list?

2. In what ways have you morphed your faith into something you do for God more than something he does for and within you?

3. List ten ways God has been loyal to you. If you can't think of any, start with your shoes and work your way up.

4. How convinced are you of God's loyalty to you? Have you interpreted some of life's twists and turns as God's disloyalty?

5. Can you name some surprising ways God has provided for your needs? Can you say he has provided all your needs?

6. What does Romans 8:38–39 say about the permanence of God's love?

Secret
#5

Endurance

The faith of Christ offers no buttons to push for quick service. The new order must wait the Lord's own time, and that is too much for the man in a hurry. He just gives up and becomes interested in something else.

—A. W. Tozer

Complaint-Free Waiting

Keep faith with God in the in-between times because, for God, time is not a complication in the achievement of your dreams.

Every parent vividly recalls humiliating episodes of screaming offspring in the most awkward settings. We can share our war stories, such as the nonstop screamfest on the cross-country flight, or the toddler's hissy fit at a funeral, or the temper tantrum in line for a TSA screening—complete with projectile vomit, which was then slimed across the floor by every subsequent would-be traveler.

I am the proud father of two great kids. As great as they are today, they were *difficult* as babies. Colicky and strong-willed. A sign of future genius, we assured ourselves.

My wife, Margi, and I ventured into the wild—i.e., the world outside our doors—with great trepidation. Dining out morphed into a high-stress operation, on the order of a military campaign.

Upon planting our firstborn in the high chair and setting our second-born's baby carrier in the booth, we informed our table server as follows: "Hi [insert name]. We have two ticking time bombs here. We don't want them screaming, your patrons don't want them screaming, and you don't want them screaming. Please help us." Our crazed expressions nicely conveyed the message: This pair is one delayed fruit cup from going postal.

We ordered immediately—sometimes before we even sat down. We brought our own crayon box, not trusting the diner's hard, waxy freebies. We asked for grapes and lemon wedges (yes) to be delivered STAT. And, no, please don't serve our courses at a leisurely pace; bring out the salad with the entrée with the dessert.

When food hit the table, we asked for the check.

When the check hit the table, we handed over the credit card.

When it came back, I added the tip and signed the slip while simultaneously shoveling food into my face, entertaining the baby, and ooh-aahing over my daughter's art creation.

We were a lean, mean, hurry-up machine.

Time was limited. The clock was running down faster than the national debt was running up. At any moment, either child could blow, meriting us the annoyed looks of peevish diners, and making the vein on my forehead throb in rhythm with the piped-in music.

The slightest delay became occasion for weeping and gnashing of teeth. And I'm not talking about the kids.

We couldn't wait.

Tick, tick, tick.

What's taking so long?

Hurry up!

Tick.

You're ruining our night out!

Complaint-Free Waiting

God takes his own sweet time.

Maybe that's because he's very, very old. Or perhaps because time means something different to him than it does to us. In either case, our earthly insistence that he hurry up the meal makes no difference at all in the pace of heaven's kitchen.

And so we wait, while all our emotional time bombs, real and imaginary, tick, tick, tick.

This requires in us the rarified character trait called endurance.

Do not let your mind drift to endless children's piano recitals, or nights wasted gluing foam balls together for back-to-school projects. Endurance is more than that. You do not get to pat yourself on the back for not losing it at the airport security line, or for not giving the DMV worker a piece of your [slowly vanishing] mind. That kind of endurance is expected. Normal people suck it up and get by.

To "grin and bear it" is not endurance.

True endurance is the ongoing choice to meet every trial with inward strength without giving up hope. It is a relentless pursuit of good—and of God—in life's storms, even while you wait for Someone to show up and calm the seas.

Joseph endured. He waited in prison for a crime he didn't commit, in a land he didn't belong to, for a dream he didn't ask for, and never lost hope.

He waited, and while he waited, he didn't complain. Nor did he fret, manipulate, lash out, pout, quit, or—most important of all—turn against God.

Joseph put on a clinic for complaint-free waiting, putting flesh on endurance, the fifth secret to a happy life.

Five Rules When You Have to Wait

It came to pass after these things that the butler and the baker of the king of Egypt offended their lord, the king of Egypt. And Pharaoh was angry with his two officers, the chief butler and the chief baker. So he put them in custody in the house of the captain of the guard, in the prison, the place where Joseph was confined. And the captain of the guard charged Joseph with them, and he served them; so they were in custody for a while.

Genesis 40:1–4

Rule #1: *Waiting isn't permission to do nothing; it's God's call to represent him today by serving others as Christ served you.*

Joseph was a prisoner, but he was a working prisoner. He manned up to the situation so much that the warden handed over the prison keys. One day, two new prison-mates joined the chain gang: Pharaoh's chief butler and chief baker. The captain of the guard appointed Joseph to be with them and to care for them. As royal servants, they were VIPs, and the captain wanted someone trustworthy to keep an eye on them.

"Stick close," he said.

"Yessir," Joseph said.

But Joseph went beyond the call of duty. He didn't just stay with them, he *served* them, the Bible says.

Instead of complaining, fretting, moping, whining, criticizing, finding fault, bellyaching, sniveling, carping, making a stink, and pouting, Joseph found his deep happiness in serving other people, even in prison.

Endurance soars high above backing into a corner and gritting your teeth till the clarinet solo is over.

Joseph endured his heartaches with dignity, poise, and hope.

And with service for God, in the meantime.

Your turn.

You might be waiting for a marriage proposal, or an operation, or a job offer, or a graduation, or to have kids, or for your kids to move out, or to hear back about the résumés you sent out. Whatever you are waiting for, realize that waiting does not mean slamming on the brakes, stopping cold, or putting your life on hold and licking your wounds.

Consider the ultimate man with the ultimate dream: Jesus. Promised glory beyond description, riches, honor, and praise, the King of kings demonstrated like no other what it means to wait.

Picture him wrapping a threadbare towel around his waist. Filling a basin. Stooping. Slipping off his disciple's sandals. Ignoring the protest. Meeting a perplexed gaze with his own serene smile. Imagine him washing the dust and grunge from gnarled feet. Toweling them dry. Moving on to the next disciple.

In all of this, he never felt smaller, never doubted his great dignity, and never lost sight of his mind-boggling destiny.

Jesus saw a direct link between service and reward. Like Joseph, almost two millennia earlier, Jesus saw no contradiction between humble service and a future throne. He never did a menial action—never embraced a child, never touched a leper, never blessed an outcast—without sensing the deep nobility of the act.

While it feels like slavery on earth, in heaven it is glory to wipe a child's snotty nose, to launder the bed sheets for those you love, to push a shopping cart through the den of psychos masquerading as a discount megamart.

We isolate greatness from service. Jesus wove them into the same cloth: "If I then, your Lord and Teacher, have washed your feet, you also ought to wash one another's feet" (John 13:14).

Rule #2: While you wait for God's promotion, keep pointing others to God and his grace.

Then the butler and the baker of the king of Egypt, who were confined in the prison, had a dream, both of them, each man's dream in one night and each man's dream with its own interpretation. And Joseph came in to them in the morning and looked at them, and saw that they were sad. So he asked Pharaoh's officers who were with him in the custody of his lord's house, saying, "Why do you look so sad today?" And they said to him, "We each have had a dream, and there is no interpreter of it." So Joseph said to them, "Do not interpretations belong to God? Tell them to me, please."

Genesis 40:5–8

I sat with a gentleman after a church service, listening to his troubles, waiting to pray for him. One of our church's prayer team members joined me. As the man described his struggles, he wept. Through his sobs, he told me and my prayer partner, "I'm in such pain, you just can't understand."

I don't want to be harsh, and my heart felt this man's pain, but there was something about his "You don't understand" that raised some red flags.

I thought of my own struggles and losses. This gentleman had no idea what I could or could not understand.

I thought of the prayer team member sitting beside me. A lifetime missionary, now retired. A twisted and crippled body. A permanent limp. He had no idea what she understood.

Yet the sobbing man couldn't see beyond his own pain.

I've indulged my own bouts with self-pity enough to sympathize, so I could be gentle with this man. But this truth remains, if you're mature enough to receive it: *You do not need to validate your own sufferings by invalidating the sufferings of others.*

When Joseph, who suffered greatly, saw his prison-mates, he paid attention to their pain. He noticed their upset; his heart went out to them. These servants of Pharaoh had dreams that unleashed a storm in their hearts.

Only God can calm a storm.

In walked God's man.

I love how Joseph got out of his own little self-absorbed orbit and asked them what was wrong. And when they answered, he didn't come back with "Mine's worse."

A miracle.

The captain made Joseph their *companion.* But Joseph made himself their *servant.* He heard their woes and made the most important statement in the paragraph: "Do not interpretations belong to God?"

He spotlighted God.

Joseph dreamed of greatness. In his dreams, his escalator only went up. Up, above his brothers. Up, above his mother and father. Up, all the way to the top.

Unfortunately, nobody with even one foot in reality would graph Joseph's life on an upward trajectory. His life plummeted downward faster than an Olympic bobsled team. Down into a pit. Down into Egypt. Down into slavery. And down into prison.

If anybody had the right to complain, it was Joseph: *God, your dreams are unreliable. When you tell me you're lifting me up, I'm packing my bags for whatever's down. I have been faithful. But all of the evidence of my life confirms my suspicion that you do not keep your promises. You give a dream and don't fulfill it. You give a dream and drive your servant in the opposite direction.*

That's what the cynical, bitter, wounded side of me might say.

Instead, Joseph pointed his buddies to God. He honored God. *Guys, there is an invisible God who holds the future in his hands, and I believe in him and you can too. And he knows dreams!*

People need hope. The headlines don't help. The job market is in the tank. Marriages are crumbling. Homeowners are upside down on their mortgages, and all our politicians can do is point fingers at each other. The impenetrable mysteries of economics and government tower over us mortals like Goliath over David.

Who has something good to say?

Who has real hope to offer?

And who can back up their message of hope with a proven endurance in the face of unrelenting stress?

You can.

Yes, you.

So Joseph honored God and invited his fellow prisoners to share their dreams.

Rule #3: *While waiting for your dreams, keep pursuing grace boldly through every avenue you can.*

First up: the butler. He dreamed of a grapevine with three branches, dripping wine into Pharaoh's cup (Genesis 40:9–13). Joseph provided the happy interpretation: in three days the butler would get his job back.

Knowing the butler represented only one degree of separation from Egypt's Pharaoh, and picturing him standing in Pharaoh's court in just three short days, Joseph tacked on a revealing plea:

> But remember me when it is well with you, and please show kindness [Hebrew, *hesed*] to me; make mention of me to Pharaoh, and get me out of this house. For indeed I was stolen away from the land of the Hebrews; and also I have done nothing here that they should put me into the dungeon.
>
> Genesis 40:14–15

He asked for "kindness." The Hebrew word, *hesed,* is one of the central biblical words for *grace.* It indicates loving-kindness, undeserved favor, and a love that is strong and steadfast.

When Joseph asked for *hesed*, he joined a small club of biblical heroes with the moxie to pursue grace:

- Jacob wrestled God, gave up fighting, and said, "I will not let you go unless you bless me" (Genesis 32:26).
- Rahab, the harlot of Jericho who protected Israel's spies, said, "Swear to me by the Lord, since I have shown you kindness [hesed], that you also will show kindness [hesed] to my father's house . . ." (Joshua 2:12).
- Abraham's servant, sent to find a bride for Isaac, prayed, "O Lord God of my master Abraham, please give me success this day, and show kindness [hesed] to my master Abraham" (Genesis 24:12).

In sales there's a ploy called "the assumptive close." The salesperson says, "Can I put you down for the red one or the blue one?" assuming either way you'll be a buyer. It's a gutsy move by a salesperson willing to risk being labeled pushy.

To ask for grace is like saying, "I would like to ask you for what I haven't earned and don't deserve. May I put you down for one dozen or two?" It's being borderline pushy when you don't have the slimmest of rights.

Sometimes people are afraid to ask for grace. Too timid. Too self-deprecating. Too proud. Too gun-shy.

While waiting for your dreams, keep pursuing grace boldly through every avenue you can.

Why? Because it's proof you haven't given up on your dreams.

There's a massive difference between contentment and settling for a sub-par status quo. Do not confuse contentment with the fine—but depressing—art of lowering your expectations. Contentment means seeking the best out of your life and never giving up on your dreams.

Missionary and sage Oswald Chambers wrote:

> People say they are tired of life; no man was ever tired of life. The truth is that we are tired of being half dead while we are alive.[1]

That half-dead zombie-state is the inevitable consequence of petering out on your dreams and abandoning your pursuit of grace.

You are eternal.

Don't let time beat you.

Joseph didn't settle. He wanted out of prison. He didn't give up on his dreams. He didn't let himself grow comfortable with a halfhearted status quo.

So far, the butler's dream sequence was looking pretty good.

Rule #4: Resist the temptation to edit God.

Second up: the baker. He dreamed of birds eating baked goods from baskets on his head (Genesis 40:16–17). If this were a movie, the soundtrack would turn ominous and dark. No good news in sight here: Dream-meister Joseph only foresaw a carcass pecked clean by scavenging birds and a dismembered head bouncing down a nearby hill.

D-Day for the baker in three . . . two . . . one . . . days.

I'm a preacher; in a sense, so was Joseph. God's message to the butler was good news, but his message to the baker was bad news. Like a waiter delivering food from the kitchen, Joseph's job was to deliver God's message to the table without messing with it.

Any good preacher should preach good news when there's good news to preach and bad news when there's bad news to preach. That's what Joseph did.

He didn't edit God.

He didn't upgrade God's image.

He let God be God, even in the bad times, even when there was no good news.

He didn't tone down God's message, though it was difficult, and though it would create unpleasant chemistry in Egypt's Alcatraz for the next three days. It's tempting to sugarcoat bad news for the sake of God's reputation. It's easy to minimize the pain as if that somehow could maximize God's glory.

Whether your waiting produces good news or bad news, it's God's news and we are not to mess with it.

Joseph let God be God.

So will anyone who waits for God's timing. To show endurance is to bow before the supremacy of your Maker. It is to allow his purposes to work in his own way, in his own time. It is to keep faith with God when outcomes seem uncertain, unpleasant, undesirable, and unwelcome.

Like an archer drawing a bow, we feel God has stretched us more than we can bear. We pray, "Lord, let go!" But he draws the bow farther. We say, "Lord, I can't take any more." He seems not to listen, and draws even farther, stretching us beyond all we imagined.

Does he not care?

Of course he cares. But we imagine he is aiming only yards away, when, in truth, he is aiming at the moon.

Joseph resisted the urge to spin the butler's pain into daisies and candy corn. He didn't edit God.

Rule #5: Never forget that you do not experience the passing of time the same way God does.

Now it came to pass on the third day, which was Pharaoh's birthday, that he made a feast for all his servants; and he lifted up the head of the chief butler and of the chief baker among his servants. Then he restored the chief butler to his butlership again, and he placed the cup in Pharaoh's hand. But he hanged the chief baker, as Joseph had interpreted to them. Yet the chief butler did not remember Joseph, but forgot him.

Genesis 40:20–23

Eight minutes spent watching a close Super Bowl finish feels wildly different from eight minutes spent waiting for a hungry toddler's smiley-fries at a diner. That's because waiting throws time into low gear and stretches it beyond all crazy-making bounds. Minutes drag on as the thing you're waiting for fills the horizon. Nothing else matters. It's like being served an undercooked steak at a steak house, and then waiting for the re-fire as your friends finish their meals. The conversation stops mattering. All that matters is how freakishly long it takes to cook a steak right. Panic sets in. *Will I get my steak back in time to enjoy the meal with my friends?*

Deadlines.

Toddler bombs.

Tick. Tick. Tick.

What if Joseph dies before anyone springs him from prison?

What if the turkey is finished before the potatoes start boiling?

What if the opportunity vanishes before the contract is signed?

What if the phone never rings for date number two?

What if the connecting flight leaves before my delayed flight lands?

We experience time as a limited commodity. For us, time's arrow cannot be reversed. Like water under a bridge, it's gone. The acids that churn your stomach lining, the muscles that constrict your lower back, the tension that squeezes your head like a vise, and the stress that makes you lash out at your family, kick the cat, and turn a cold shoulder to God, are symptoms of an urgency arising from the awareness that your days are numbered.

— Precious life marches toward the grave even while you're mired in this hellhole of a prison. Meanwhile, the only people who can help you either: a) loathe you, b) think you're dead, c) paint you as a criminal, d) think you deserve it, e) have forgotten you, or f) are too busy with their own futures.

God does not experience time as we do.

To us, time is a succession of events. First this, then that, then the next thing. Moment by moment slips by like a stream; then it's over. One life-span. Seventy, ninety, a hundred years. Who knows? One life-span and it's over.

For us, time is precious and irretrievable. And every moment that goes by without us in our ultimate dream lives is a moment wasted, never to be recovered.

Your soul knows this.

Unless you have an alternative, your soul panics.

Here's the alternative.

For God, time is different. He inhabits eternity. For him, time is not a succession of events; rather, he comprehends all of time as one indivisible, singular moment. This is called the eternity (or eternality) of God. One scholar defines it as:

> . . . that perfection of God whereby He is elevated above all temporal limits and all succession of moments, and possesses the whole of His existence in one indivisible present.[2]

"From everlasting to everlasting," he is God (Psalm 90:2). He is the "High and Lofty One Who inhabits eternity" (Isaiah 57:15).

When you walk with God and feel your time wasting away and opportunities slipping by—when you languish in the prison house of unmet dreams and unsatisfied expectations—remember this:

For God, time is eternal.

For God, time is reversible.

For God, time is extendable.

For God, time is recoverable.

For God, the passage of time is not a complication in the achievement of your dreams.

- When Joshua needed more time to fight a battle, God made the sun stand still (Joshua 10:13).

- When Joel needed more time to recover from national stupidity, God restored the years that the locust had eaten (Joel 2:25).
- When King Hezekiah needed more time to live for God, God lengthened his life by fifteen years (2 Kings 20:6).

Be at peace. God can handle the big bully called Time. He's bigger than it.

To whatever degree you have placed your life in God's hand, for you time's inexorable march is never an emergency. You have plenty of it. Lots and lots of it. You've got an infinity of it.

When it comes to waiting, we are all too often children demanding our smiley-fries now.

Only the mature Christ-follower can wait for God's time, enduring without complaining, drawing happiness from a source time's passage can't ruin.

God Doesn't Forget

Yes, the butler forgot Joseph. But God didn't. The prophet Isaiah painted a touching picture of a mother and her infant. He asked,

Can a woman forget her nursing child, and not have compassion on the son of her womb? Surely they may forget, yet I will not forget you. See, I have inscribed you on the palms of my hands. . . .

Isaiah 49:15–16

Why can't God forget you? Because you draw moment by moment sustenance from him. Why can't he forget you? Because he has inscribed you on the palms of his hands. The nail-scarred hands of Jesus become a constant reminder of his love.

Though you think you drown in a sea of forgetfulness, your Father in heaven remembers.

Don't quit. Don't grow weary. Endure hardship. A better day is coming.

Your Deliverer is on his way.

S . . . L . . . O . . . W . . . L . . . Y . . .

For Reflection and Discussion

1. How good are you at waiting? What's the worst part of it? Have you ever lost your temper while waiting?

2. What are some big things you wish God would hurry up in your life? How would you describe your attitude toward those delays?

3. List some differences between a "grin and bear it" philosophy and biblical endurance.

4. What do you think time feels like to God?

5. How do you feel when you have to ask for help, charity, or grace? Is it demeaning to pursue grace from God? From others?

6. Read Joshua 10:13, Joel 2:25, and 2 Kings 20:6 along with the surrounding contexts. What do these passages imply about God's power over time?

Secret
6

Trust

Providences are long chains with many links in them. If one link were missing, the event would fail. But it is God's chain and God's plan. The thing is fixed. The outcome is not doubtful.

—William S. Plumer (1802–1880)

Faith in a Successful God

Rest in the providence of God, because your happiness depends on trusting a God who simply cannot fail.

* * *

You might not know that Domino Day falls on November 15. On that day in 2008, the Weijers Domino Productions team set a world record.[1] They triggered a chain reaction toppling 4,345,027 dominoes.

Records within the record included:

- Longest domino spiral (200 meters)
- Highest domino climb (12 meters)

- Longest domino wall (16 meters)
- Largest domino structure (25,000 stones)
- Largest rectangular level domino field (1 million stones)

The production team actually set up 4.5 million dominos, but due to accidental gaps, over 100,000 dominoes didn't fall.

A sophisticated rigging system allowed builders to "fly" above their work-in-progress. This permitted a bird's-eye view of the project, and provided easy access within the complex structure.

As part of construction, the builders used "safeties." Safeties consisted either of gaps in the line of dominoes or of physical barriers. That way if a domino toppled by accident, the whole project didn't have to start over.[2]

Spacing meant everything. A 2009 attempt to break the record failed when a number of stones were set too far apart to topple their sections.

Is a domino building career in your future? The production company periodically hires new builders. The main requirements are "steady hands, infinite patience, immunity to stress, and being able to concentrate for long periods of time."[3] Do you qualify?

God does.

What looks like God's forgetfulness may just mean that your section of the cosmic domino project hasn't toppled yet.

Not Forgotten

While Joseph slaved away in prison, the butler luxuriated in the palace of the king. His white-collar job offered great perks: food from Pharaoh's table, wine from his cellars, refreshing evenings in the royal swimming pool, visions of the harem, and opulence enough to make Donald Trump salivate.

In the affairs of life, the only person in Egypt who might possibly help Joseph forgot him.

So God, with a flick of his omniscient fingertip, shoved over a domino.

This triggered a disturbing dream for Pharaoh; he was not happy. When Pharaoh wasn't happy, nobody was happy. Like all spoiled rich kids, he transmitted his personal drama to the entire household.

This, in turn, triggered a memory in the distracted mind of our forgetful butler: There was a really good dream-guy doing time in the federal penitentiary. He spoke up:

> Now there was a young Hebrew man with us there, a servant of the captain of the guard. And we told him, and he interpreted our dreams for us; to each man he interpreted according to his own dream. And it came to pass, just as he interpreted for us, so it happened. He restored me to my office, and he hanged him.
>
> Genesis 41:12–13

The dominoes are falling.

In rapid-fire succession, Joseph will leave prison, interpret Pharaoh's dream, take a priestly wife, and step up to the second most powerful position in all the mighty empire of Egypt. Yes, this is a great success for Joseph.

But Joseph's success is not the deepest message.

God's success is.

In case you haven't caught on yet, I'm doing all I can to help you anchor your happiness in God. If a good and gracious God fills your horizon, how can you not be happy?

When Joseph's dominoes have fallen, they will culminate in a breathtakingly satisfying conclusion. No one could have predicted the twists and turns by which God made his dreams come true—a thousand times better than he could have imagined or orchestrated himself.

And you, when you replay your life's twists and turns on heaven's monitors, will gasp at the jaw-dropping arrangements of a God who does all things well.

I wish I could promise every reader great health and wealth on planet earth. I can't; God doesn't.

Happiness is a treasure money can't buy.

You may never have riches. You may never have fame. You may never publish a book, have your face on the cover of a glamour magazine, win *American Idol,* dance in public, or finish a marathon. You may look at others, far less deserving than you, who enjoy far greater riches and far better health than you've ever dreamed of.

You wonder why. When is your day coming? What is God doing? For every Joseph who gets sprung from prison, ten thousand never see the light of day again.

What gives?

What gives is a God who is able to deliver happiness to a soul, no matter your health, wealth, or circumstance.

What gives is a God who sees beyond time's horizon into a forever where earthly treasures fade into nothingness, and what matters is the great imperishable crown of faithfulness.

God keeps his promises. He can do anything but fail. Joseph will ride God's wave all the way to the top. But don't miss the simple point that it is God's wave. It is God's work, God's power, and God's wisdom that composes the story to an enormously satisfying resolution.

But he plays hide-and-seek while he does it.

Providence

Our Christian grandparents knew something we don't: They rested in the providence of God. It's too bad the word *providence* has evaporated from the Christian vocabulary. It's the background music to our lives with God.

When Pharaoh retrieved Joseph from prison, who did that: Pharaoh or God?

When he set Joseph on the throne of Egypt (coming soon), who did that: Pharaoh or God?

When Joseph stored up surplus food during seven years of plenty, and when he released it during seven years of famine—preserving innumerable lives and bringing honor to his God—who did that: Joseph or God?

Providence describes the beautiful but often tricky dance between the will of God and the free-will choices of people like Pharaoh, Joseph, and us.

Once you understand God's providence, you never see yourself in the same way again. I'd like to offer a simple definition first, and then a more technical one.

SIMPLE: Providence is God's way of shepherding our lives and our world to fulfill his beautiful purposes.

TECHNICAL: This one comes from a famous theology expert: "Providence may be defined as that continued exercise of the divine energy whereby the Creator preserves all His creatures, is operative in all that comes to pass in the world, and directs all things to their appointed end."[4]

Providence is the ongoing guardianship God exercises over all he has made, including you. He is not distant, not aloof, and not indifferent. God is intimately involved in all details of your life, even the minor ones, like how many hairs remain on your thinning scalp (Luke 12:7).

Your life is not subject to the whims of luck, fate, chance, or karma. You are not at the mercy of the stars or their alignments. Superstition, bad juju, the evil eye, and so-called past-life failures cannot haunt you. Not even the randomness of an indiscriminate, materialistic universe controls you.

Your life is in the hands of a caring, merciful, wise, holy, all-powerful God. He calls the shots—even when you're positive he has called them wrong. Even when you don't believe in God. Or when you say you don't believe in God. He's in charge. Impersonal forces beyond your control lie easily in the grip of his hand.

We rest our anxious hearts in the providence of God; we do not resign ourselves to *Que Sera Sera* (with apologies to Doris Day) or wring our hands over today's horoscope.

Our heavenly Father is working every hour of every day, in, around, and through our lives, for our benefit and good (Romans 8:28).

I know this raises troubling questions about God's involvement in evil—could there be a better case study than the life of Joseph?

In our technical definition, providence stands on a three-legged stool.

- PRESERVATION: "The Creator preserves all his creatures."
- CONCURRENCE (also called COOPERATION): God "is operative in all that comes to pass in the world."
- GOVERNMENT: He "directs all things to their appointed ends."

Rather than a dry academic dissertation on what all this means, let's leap back into Joseph's story to see how these three elements play out.

Preservation

If God stopped willing it, you would cease to exist before you finished your next breath. If God stopped willing it, the molecules of oxygen picked up in your lungs by molecules of hemoglobin in your blood would fail in their duty, and you would die from oxygen deprivation.

Preservation means that God holds the universe together. He keeps planets spinning, quarks wiggling, synapses firing, and photons hurtling.

Through preservation, worms crawl through dirt, birds fly on the winds, and gravity keeps us all from flying into space.

Through preservation, the hydrologic cycle sends moisture upward and rains downward. The sun heats the planet, and photosynthesis keeps things green.

Except in time of drought. Like the one Egypt was going to face.

If God interrupted the laws of physics every time somebody wanted him to, our necks would be sore from getting thrown back and forth in a rickety roller coaster of an unpredictable universe. The laws of physics would go *poof!* and we'd be stuck guessing every day if the sun would rise.

Or if the cheese would melt on the pizza.

No, preservation is the only way to go.

Thank God he keeps the universe and the laws of physics humming along smoothly. Whatever properties he wove into your being when he made you, he upholds as well. Dogs bark because of God. Fish swim because of God. And butlers and bakers dream because of God.

His people once sang:

> You alone are the LORD; you have made heaven, the heaven of heavens, with all their host, the earth and everything on it, the seas and all that is in them, and you preserve them all. The host of heaven worships you.
>
> Nehemiah 9:6

This doesn't mean that God is the direct cause of everything that happens—especially of sin—but it does mean that what God has made continually does what God made it to do. For better or worse, richer or poorer, in sickness and in health, till death do us part.

Concurrence

> Then Pharaoh sent and called Joseph, and they brought him quickly out of the dungeon; and he shaved, changed his clothing, and came to Pharaoh.
>
> Genesis 41:14

In 1997, a beautiful woman walked across a classroom where I—an unmarried young pastor—was teaching at Wednesday night Bible study. She was classy, sexy, beautiful, and confident. The mystery woman pulled up a seat next to my lifelong friend, Denise, a young woman in my church. I don't have the slightest clue what kind of babbling I did for the next hour as the Bible class teacher, because I was smitten.

As it turned out, my future bride walked into my life that night. Later, Denise explained that Margi was not only her friend but also her boss—an attorney with a great reputation for excellence and integrity.

Dominoes fell.

Who did that?

Perhaps Denise, our mutual friend, did that; she was the indispensable link in the chain that brought Margi to my church. Maybe Margi did that. She's the one who endured a forty-five-minute commute that night to show up at Bible class. You could say that I did it, because I showed up too, ready to teach and win her over with wit, intelligence, humor, and stellar good looks.

Or not.

Providence teaches something deeper and far more wonderful: God brought us together. God himself, working in and through our choices, brooded over a plan and hatched it at just the right time. Just as God promoted Joseph through Pharaoh, God brought Margi and me together. And here is the mind-blowing factoid: He wove our free-will choices into the accomplishment of his perfect plan. We didn't feel coerced or manipulated by God. We wanted each other, freely. It was our choice.

But it was God's choice too.

In the beautiful language of theology, God *concurred* or *co-operated* with our choices. Like a hand in a glove, God is the invisible co-actor in all that comes to pass. Two parties act together, in concert, their actions converging even when their intentions diverge. What one party means for evil, another means for good. Whether rain falls, winds blow, butlers forget, or Pharaohs dream, God is there.

The genius and power of God blazes forth in his incomparable ability to bring good out of evil. God is not the author of evil; he can't be (James 1:13). But his grace-filled heart has mastered the art of converting the freely chosen evil of his subjects into the freely bestowed blessings we never saw coming.

Whether a sparrow falls, an innocent boy gets sold to slaves, or a world-class beauty walks across the back of a Bible class, for his own purposes, and in his own way, God has his fingers in the pie, and he's cooking up something delicious.

If you accept the premise of God's great mercy, you cannot consider the truth of divine concurrence without an overwhelming sense of comfort. I feel safe with this God—even when on the surface he seems far away. The Bible calls him *Yahweh Shammah*, the Lord Who Is There (Ezekiel 48:35).

He was there when I was single and lonely, there when we lost a much-wanted child through miscarriage, there when our retirement account went *poof*, there when my son needed surgery, there when a loved one got unsettling medical news, there when my daughter wept over another year of braces, and there when my courageous dad battled his fifth cancer.

God's always there. He's always working, connecting, enabling each creature to do its thing, permitting free will to run its course, holding evil in its bounds, giving us our choices and not always shielding us from the consequences.

When the Bible says Joseph got a makeover and was hustled before Pharaoh, you get the idea a whole lot more is going on than meets the eye.

God did that, through concurrence, the second leg on providence's three-legged stool.

Government

Then Joseph said to Pharaoh, "The dreams of Pharaoh are one; God has shown Pharaoh what he is about to do."

Genesis 41:25

C. S. Lewis observed, "History is a story written by the finger of God." Like children on a field trip, every atom and subatomic particle, every bolt of lightning and falling leaf, every person, angel, place, and thing, reaches its proper destination through the faithful oversight of God. He "works all things according to the counsel of his will" (Ephesians 1:11).

History is not random. Today's desperate headlines are not disconnected bits of bad luck floating on a sea of randomness. They are, rather, the outworking of a beautiful plan from the beautiful mind of God. The fact that we cannot appreciate his plan—or that we kick against it or even resent it—only shows our shrimp-sized imaginations before the infinitely exquisite will of God.

When God denied other applicants the job and made my friend, Denise, a certain attorney's assistant, he was governing history to bring me my bride—and now my very own personal attorney. Only by the inscrutable wisdom of God can everyone come out a winner—even the applicants who didn't get Denise's job. God was working a plan to bless them too, if they were open to it.

In theology, *government* does not refer to politicians sponging off taxpayers. It refers to how God unfolds history so his will is done on earth as it is in heaven. He governs all things to their proper ends.

When history's fireworks are complete, you and I, along with angels and the rest of the cosmos, will spontaneously burst into thunderous applause, leaping for joy and shouting our praise for a finale ten thousand times better than we ever dared dream.

You will stand in stunned amazement, realizing that what looked like *accidents* were God's intentions, perfectly woven into his design. What looked like *evil*, God overcame by his design. What looked like *undeserved suffering*, God repaid countless times over by his design—so it will be worth it all when we see Jesus. What looked like getting away with *sin*, God caught up with in his design, inflicting a manifestly righteous punishment. What looked like a *sad ending*, God transformed by his design into the happily-ever-after your heart always longed for.

I vote God for governor of the cosmos.

And of my life and world.

Are you with me? Will you trust him when the bad stuff happens? Will you keep faith with the God who's never let you down? Will you praise him in good times and in bad? Will you bless the Lord in adversity, understanding he's only setting up dominoes for a glorious chain reaction?

Adversity is inevitable but misery is optional. It is optional precisely because the Ruler of All Things has your best interests in mind. If that doesn't make you happy, what will?

Maybe it's time to peel away our tightly clenched fingers from our need to control everything. I vote God for governor. Can he count on your vote too?

I imagine Joseph voted that way too. And now, through Joseph, God even wins the vote of Egypt's Pharaoh.

Pharaoh's eyes grew wide, and he stroked his carefully man-scaped goatee, as Joseph predicted seven years of plenty followed by seven years of famine. He nodded sagely as Joseph offered a plan: Store up 20 percent of the grain per year for the seven good years, and sell it off during the seven bad years. He then scrunched up his royal nose and puzzled over Joseph's final suggestion: Pick a really smart, dependable, proven, get-it-done guy to head the operation. Ahem. Ahem.

The Part of the Story Where Dreams Come True

So the advice was good in the eyes of Pharaoh and in the eyes of all his servants. And Pharaoh said to his servants, "Can we find such a one as this, a man in whom is the Spirit of God?" Then Pharaoh said to Joseph, "Inasmuch as God has shown you all this, there is no one as discerning and wise as you. You shall be over my house, and all my people shall be ruled according to your word; only in regard to the throne will I be greater than you."

Genesis 41:37–40

Consider the astonishing chain reaction that ushered Joseph to the throne of Egypt. If you asked him, "Hey Joseph, how did you get to be the ruler in Egypt?" he would say . . .

- It started with this jacket—a coat of many colors, and . . .
- My brothers hated me, so . . .
- They threw me in a pit. They were going to murder me, but . . .
- They sold me to foreign slave traders instead. Thus . . .
- I served as a slave in Egypt, unfortunate but necessary so that . . .

- My master's wife could frame me and . . .
- I'd get thrown in jail. This was also unfortunate, but necessary, because . . .
- Two other prisoners came from Pharaoh's court with their dreams, and I had to interpret them because . . .
- The butler went back to Pharaoh's courts, and years later, Pharaoh had a dream, so the butler remembered me, and . . .
- Bada-bing, here I am, the lord and master of all Egypt, second only to Pharaoh himself, so that, in God's grand design, I might . . .
- Save hundreds of thousands from death by starvation, and point a searching world to the invisible God of heaven . . . all of which makes me . . .
- Deeply happy.

Dominoes.

Remove even a single domino, the stack doesn't fall, and hosts of people die. God, by his providence, is hard at work, even when he feels a million miles away. You can rest your anxious heart in the jaw-dropping providence of God.

That doesn't guarantee an easy life.

Just look at the chain reaction that brought Joseph to the throne. No sane person would choose any of it. You would pray against it, fight against it, work against it, and lobby against it—every single step.

Like a mom bringing her child for vaccinations, someone else had to choose it or it wouldn't happen.

Consider God your gigantic Someone Else.

The tough times have meaning. God knows.

You ask him why, but he doesn't answer.

Maybe that's because of the size of our brains relative to his; trying to explain every trial would be like explaining vaccinations—or particle physics—to a toddler.

Or maybe God doesn't answer because of his deep fondness for faith.

I don't know. I'm just glad I'm not the one setting up the dominoes.

Pharaoh said, "I hear you interpret dreams."

Joseph said, "It is not in me; God will give Pharaoh an answer of peace" (Genesis 41:16).

What did Joseph have in his heart to honor God so well?

He had "that sweet, inward, quiet, gracious frame of spirit, which freely submits to and delights in God's wise and fatherly disposal in every condition."

God's Worst Best Day

Imagine the darkness of the day Jesus Christ hung on the cross. By appearances, all hope was lost. God had failed; the purpose of God was thwarted. No words could capture the demonic glee as the Son of God breathed his last. God failed! Or so the demons thought. Even the disciples gave up.

But God says, "So shall my word be that goes forth from my mouth; it shall not return to me void, but it shall accomplish what I please, and it shall prosper in the thing for which I sent it" (Isaiah 55:11).

God cannot fail. God will not fail. His words are unstoppable. His counsel is irresistible. His providence accounts for every detail, potentiality, free-will choice, and sub-atomic wiggle. The cross was the defeat of neither God nor of Jesus. It was the defeat of Satan. It just took a while for the devil to figure it out.

But what is a three-day wait in the span of eternity?

Though you wait beyond endurance, and though life falls apart, never give up. The Occupant of heaven's throne is on your side. He will not be late with his blessing. He never fails to accomplish his purposes. Bank on it.

Whether your victory arrives on the third day or in the thirtieth year, what is that in the span of eternity?

Jesus, in a final, gasping breath, cried out, "It is finished."

What was finished?

The entirety of God's work to cleanse sinners from their sin; that's what was finished. Jesus, by himself, accomplished in three dark hours on the cross what countless sacrifices piled on top of innumerable good deeds could never do. He opened the door to forgiveness. He paid a price we could never pay. He effected mankind's salvation and offered the gift of everlasting life to all who will believe and receive it.

Think of that word *finished*.

If salvation's work is finished, what is left for you to do? More work? More effort? More striving, sacrificing, paying, giving, performing, sweating, straining, proving, fixing, repaying, improving? Of course not. Finished means finished. Jesus meant it. I hereby set you free from all your labors trying to improve what Jesus already finished. Life with God is a *gift*, totally free, paid in full by the blood of the Savior.

I received that gift as a boy, maybe nine years old. God met me in my tiny church in Chicago, in the person of a round, perky, sweet Bible teacher we called Aunt Alice. Jesus made me his own. It stuck. Along the way I doubted, vacillated, questioned, and squirmed, but God never let me go. I'm as much God's child today as I was back then.

I was very young when I received God's gift.

Others have waited a bit longer. Some, like my dad, received God's gift in old age—in his eighties. He went to heaven not too long ago, a happy and confident man. It makes no difference *when* in life's timeline you step across the line of faith—just do it before you've drawn your last breath, because after that, it's too late.

Have you received the gift?

Have you turned from self-salvation to God's salvation through Christ? A simple yes to Jesus settles life's most troubling questions: Why are you here and where are you going and how can you make sense of it all?

Please don't wait.

When Pharaoh asked Joseph to interpret his dream, he figured Joseph would use his magical powers to conjure some spiritual mojo. Joseph set him straight: "So Joseph answered Pharaoh, saying, 'It is not in me; God will give Pharaoh an answer of peace'" (Genesis 41:16).

Not in me, but in God.

That is the nucleus of every cell in a happy life.

Providence Wins

And Pharaoh called Joseph's name Zaphnath-Paaneah. And he gave him as a wife Asenath, the daughter of Poti-Pherah priest of On. So Joseph went out over all the land of Egypt. . . . And to Joseph were born two sons before the years of famine came, whom Asenath, the daughter of Poti-Pherah priest of On, bore to him. Joseph called the name of the firstborn Manasseh: "For God has made me forget all my toil and all my father's house." And the name of the second he called Ephraim: "For God has caused me to be fruitful in the land of my affliction."

Genesis 41:45, 50–52

Your Father in heaven will take care of you. He will stop the sun, part the sea, split the mountain, demolish the walls, slay the giant, quench the fire, calm the storm, uncover the secret, bring fire from heaven, consume the sacrifice, make the lame to walk, the blind to see, the deaf to hear, and the dead to rise again if he has to.

He'll line up the dominoes. He'll shove over the dominoes. He's the Lord of chain reactions, and when we've seen the finale, we'll cheer like lunchroom kids on pizza day.

In every place Joseph went, God was with him, and that made all the difference. In the pit, the prison, or the palace—Joseph was content. Why? Because even when Joseph's environment was terrible, his *invironment*—that inner world of emotion, belief, and thought—was fit for a king.

Joseph's drama is the Bible's flesh-and-blood incarnation of:

And we know that God causes all things to work together for good to those who love God, to those who are called according to his purpose.

Romans 8:28 NASB

All things. No loose ends. No wasted tears. No unresolved chords leaving you hanging for resolution.

God causes all things. Kiss randomness good-bye. Say hello to the Lord of dominoes.

God causes all things to work together. A knit tapestry looks like chaos on the backside, beauty on the front. For now, we see all things from the backside. One day it will all make sense.

For good. Good outcomes. Good blessings. Good relationships. The path may be rocky but the destination is good.

Look at the names Joseph gave his sons: God made me forget my toil and my loss (Manasseh). God caused me to be fruitful in the land of my affliction (Ephraim). Joseph understood by age thirty what most never know: There is a God who governs the affairs in heaven above and on earth beneath, and he always has your best in mind.

The Altar Call

Maybe, like Pharaoh, your spirit is troubled. He saw enough truth to be afraid, but not enough to find peace. Is there an unsettled feeling in your heart? Have you barked up all the wrong trees for a happy life? Count it as a sign you have not yet laid the most basic foundation of all: your own personal connection with God through Christ.

As I said earlier, you may not agree with the God-talk, and I appreciate that you've stayed this far into the book. Thanks for keeping an open mind.

Here's the heart of it.

Jesus came for you, lived for you, died for you, and rose again for you. When he was on the cross, you were on his mind. He was loving you and purchasing your eternal life—your truest, deepest, most real life of all. On that cross, he absorbed the guilt and shame for every skeleton in your closet from cradle to grave. He died, legitimizing a holy God's love for moral train wrecks like you and me.

He finished his work, once for *all.*

All includes you.

Only Jesus can satisfy your soul.

Right now, Jesus waits for you with arms open wide. Run to him.

Here is a prayer you can use to express that you are opening your life to God through Jesus.

It could be that one day you'll step back in wide-eyed wonder, realizing that the day you picked up this book, a critical domino toppled, triggering this sacred moment: when you do serious business with a great God.

Prayer

Dear God,

There's an empty place in my heart that only you can fill. I've tried a million things to fill it. I've even dabbled in God-stuff—not enough to disturb my comfort, just enough to feel better for a time. Sometimes you feel out of reach. I know that's my fault, not yours.

I admit I fall short of your standards. I've messed up, failed, sinned more times than I can count.

I've done my own thing.

I've gone my own way.

I'm still not happy.

I do not deserve your love. I'm a sinner. I need a Savior. I admit it.

God, right now I'm telling you I believe Jesus is my Savior. I believe he is your Son. I believe he died on the cross for me, shedding his precious blood as my substitute. He alone did this, without my help. It is his great sacrifice, and not mine, that is my salvation. I believe Jesus alone offers me the gift of life, full and free, right now, just for the taking. I don't know exactly how it all works, but I'm telling you I believe in Jesus.

So God, right now I choose him and his gift of life, now and forever.

Right now I trust Jesus Christ, embrace him, and appoint him as my only hope. He is my only hope for forgiveness, for acceptance into your family, and for eternal life. My only hope for happiness on earth. My only hope for a place in heaven.

God, I am asking you, as best I can, right now, for Christ's sake, please save me. Embrace me. Make me your child. Forgive my sins. I officially—right here, right now—rest my life, my heart, my time and eternity on Jesus Christ and his amazing grace.

Amen.

For Reflection and Discussion

1. Have you ever heard the word *providence* before? What has it brought to mind for you?

2. In what ways would resting in God's providence contribute to your happiness?

3. What makes it hard to trust the providence of God?

4. Which element of providence (preservation, government, concurrence) is most comforting to you? Why?

5. Can you be happy with treasures money can't buy?

6. What comes to mind when you read Romans 8:28?

Secret

#**7**

Closure

No sin can be crucified either in heart or life, unless it be first pardoned in conscience, because there will be want of faith to receive the strength of Jesus, by whom alone it can be crucified. If it be not mortified in its guilt, it cannot be subdued in its power.[1]

—William Romaine, 1793

* * *

Closure for the Sins of Your Past
Close the books on unresolved guilt and shame, because those loose ends only guarantee misery.

* * *

"They call those things *tolerations*," my friend said.

"A perfect word for it," I said.

"They build up stress in you and sometimes you don't know why," he said. "But tolerations are always there, draining the life out of you."

My friend Ken is a certified life coach. He is also a very wise pastor. We were talking about some work I had done around my house. A contractor repaired our front entry door; it had never closed properly and was getting worse over time. By the time I called the repairman, it required sumo-like strength to lock it. My wife dreaded opening that door; she couldn't close it. Other doors had problems too: one wouldn't latch, another wouldn't stay open, yet another rubbed against the frame.

The contractor fixed them all. I remarked to Ken how good it felt to close the front door and turn the latch with no effort at all. I ticked off a few other nagging projects we had finally gotten to around the house, and how I felt more relieved than I'd expected.

That's when Ken told me about tolerations: that mountain of undone tasks that zaps your happiness. Every time you walk by a dead light bulb, a pesky high-achiever inside your brain whispers, "Gotta change the light bulb." You don't have time at the moment, so you let it slide—at least you *think* you let it slide. Your soul is finicky—it lets nothing slide. So you carry that duty like a needless rock in a mountain-climber's backpack.

Change the light bulb, file the receipts, clean the junk drawer, clear out the kids' outgrown clothes, defrost the freezer, organize the garage, floss the teeth, send the thank-you cards, unpack the boxes from the last move . . . like a flock of angry birds, everyday life tolerations can peck you to madness.

Add to that a whole flock of tolerations pecking your self-worth. You weigh too much. You're terminally disorganized. You snap at the kids. You've dropped out of church or haven't prayed for a long time. Your Bible sits lonely, unused, and gathering dust. Your self-worth is in the toilet.

Yet another gaggle flocks to your relationships. There's that friend you hurt, that phone call you owe, those emails you haven't answered, that Facebook comment you need to make, that half-finished project you promised your kids.

There will never be peace in your heart till you bring closure to the unfinished business of your past—especially as it relates to marriage, family, and friends. You might be able to tolerate the unfinished caulking around the stairs, but it's the unfinished guilt or the simmering bitterness that's making you a lunatic.

For twenty years, Joseph's brothers harbored a life-destroying toleration. I can only imagine how the conspiracy of silence weighed them down, draining the joy from two decades of life. Imagine the knot in their guts over the empty chair at family gatherings and the agonized creases on their father's brow.

They can't get past what they did, but they can't admit it either. So they keep the secret and live with the unfinished business of a tormented conscience.

How many people do we rub shoulders with every day that bend under a load of guilt and shame? Maybe you're there. You have failed God. You've disappointed your parents. You've hurt your children, your spouse, or your church. Like the prodigal son, you've blown your money and crossed boundaries you swore you'd never cross.

Your tolerations have made life intolerable, and you feel stuck, just like Joseph's brothers.

God is about to finish their unfinished business for them. He wants to do the same for you.

This would be a perfect time to invest fifteen minutes in reading Genesis 42 through 45. What we're going to talk about will make more sense with the background story in mind.

Thanks.

Let's review.

When worldwide famine struck, only Egypt had grain, thanks to Joseph. Joseph's father, Jacob, feeling the pinch of famine, sent his sons to Egypt to buy grain. The very men who abused Joseph bowed before him with outstretched hands.

Don't you love God's sense of humor?

Here are the highlights of this part of the tale.

Limping Beneath Your Identity

When Jacob saw that there was grain in Egypt, Jacob said to his sons, "Why do you look at one another?" And he said, "Indeed I have heard that there is grain in Egypt; go down to that place and buy for us there, that we may live and not die." So Joseph's ten brothers went down to buy grain in Egypt. But Jacob did not send Joseph's brother Benjamin with his brothers, for he said, "Lest some calamity befall him." And the sons of Israel went to buy grain among those who journeyed, for the famine was in the land of Canaan.

Genesis 42:1–5

God is making his people into spiritual royalty. It is his goal to create a tribe that rises up to their full dignity and potential—men and women who stand tall and proud as favored children of the Most High God.

This triggers all sorts of inner alarms. Your conscience claws your heart. Your emotions turn dark. Your physiology churns up excess stomach acid, an aching neck, or unusual drowsiness. Your spirit, like an eager little beaver, alternates between spasms of self-justification, self-punishment, and self-loathing.

Think Joseph's brothers.

When your *lifestyle* contradicts your *identity*, you feel crazy. A happy life is impossible in this sorry state, with the exception of a psychotically happy life—but let's not go there.

You need to quit limping beneath your own identity. God made you for better than this.

By closure I mean closing the gap you've created by flying beneath your glorious identity.

This isn't easy.

He Names You by Your Potential

When Jacob said "Egypt," no doubt his sons hung their heads like my dog when I caught him stealing donuts off the kitchen counter. They flashed back to the day slave traders dragged away their screaming little brother. Their faces turned red, their eyes look downward.

There's a powerful lesson hidden in Genesis 42:1–5; it has to do with how Joseph's brothers are identified. Here's the progression: they are called . . .

A. Jacob's sons (v. 1)

B. Joseph's brothers (v. 3)

C. Sons of Israel (v. 5)

This is no accident. Jacob's name, in its original Hebrew language, means something like *cheater*. When God met him in a special way, he renamed him Israel. Israel means something like *prince with God*.

So we have to ask this question: How will God transform these men from a) sons of a cheater into c) sons of a prince with God? The answer somehow passes through their role as b) "Joseph's brothers."

They have to put their scandal to rest.

God is assembling a royal family, and he is using these barbarians as his raw material.

If God can make a royal family out of these men, he can make a royal family out of anyone. That includes you and me on our worst days. The fact that you have sinned, even miserably, does not disqualify you from God's salvation, love, or blessings.

Yes, there may be consequences, but among them you will not find an eviction notice from the love of God.

Some people might think they've gone too far. They're convinced that not even God can bring them back. They are terminally stuck on the wrong side of a spiritual point of no return.

Think again.

The truth is wonderfully opposite: No one is beyond God's forgiveness. There is hope for the worst offenders, even these evil brothers.

This is because of God's boundless grace. He does not name you by your *failures*; he names you by your *potential*. He sees the glorious reality of who he made you to be—who you really are, right now, once he cleans away the crud piled on top of you. At this point in the story, these brothers see little potential in themselves; they stoop under the burden of unfinished business and a false sense of self.

For twenty years, whatever happiness they've had has been fleeting. Whatever joy has been spoiled by the weight of what they did.

Just watch as God helps them close the books on their gangster past.

Baggage

When the brothers made the epic trek to Egypt, they stood before the prime minister to buy grain. He just happened to be their long-lost, mortally offended brother. Joseph recognized his brothers, but they didn't recognize him.

This made for all kinds of comical irony.

Genesis 42 describes four cycles in their conversation, and it wasn't good. Joseph initiated each cycle with an accusation:

- He "spoke roughly to them" (v. 7).
- He "said to them, 'You are spies!'" (v. 9).
- "He said to them, 'No, but you have come to see the nakedness of the land!'" (v. 12).
- "Joseph said to them, 'It is as I spoke to you, saying, 'You are spies!'" (v. 14).

What was going on?

God was slapping them upside the head with a life-defining truth: *The greatest disaster that can ever happen to a human being is settling into a lifestyle beneath your true identity.*

So in his mercy, God freezes his children before the mirror of truth and bids us take a long, hard look. What might you see?

- Deception, conniving, a false front
- Bitterness, resentment, an unforgiving heart
- Revenge, passive-aggressiveness
- Evil, cruelty, meanness, abuse
- Selfishness, narcissism, self-justification, self-promotion
- Broken relationships
- Theft, greed, coveting, grasping, pleonexia
- Slander, backbiting, gossip

- Plotting
- Rebellion
- Pride, self-righteousness, religiosity, judgmentalism
- Exclusivity, racism, sexism
- Hypocrisy
- Woundedness, neediness, desperation
- Temper, rage, seething hostility
- Self-pity, self-loathing, self-destruction
- Despair, quitting, giving up

Welcome to the human race: You have baggage.

When you deny it, your baggage defines you.

When you admit it, your identity in God begins to define you.

God has a place for all that baggage: at the foot of the cross where Jesus died. Leave it there. Let it go. Jesus will carry it far away, over the ocean of God's forgiveness, and drop it into the depths of forgetfulness.

Your past need never haunt you again. It doesn't define you. It need not dominate you. Yes, there might be consequences—lasting and difficult—but they do not change your identity in Christ. You are who God says you are, no matter what the evils, losses, traumas, and bullies from the past say about you.

Until you shed the false identity crusting over your true self, your glorious true identity stays mired in the dirt.

Closure for past guilt is your birthright in the family of God.

So the brothers presented themselves before the ruler of Egypt as decent guys in need of grain. Joseph set his sights on the heavy baggage of guilt and shame they have yet to even name.

"You Are Spies"

Joseph called them spies (Genesis 42:9).

A spy is a deceptive person. A spy projects a false reality. "You guys are not what you seem to be," he said.

Joseph was right, wasn't he? They *seemed* to be decent, hard-working family men. They didn't look like murderous betrayers of their little brother. They were not as innocent as they seemed. When Joseph called them spies, he stuck his spiritual scalpel into their hypocritical hearts and gave it a twist.

Jesus told a parable about two men approaching the temple. One—a religious leader—puffed himself up and bragged to God about how lucky God was to have him on the team. The other stood at a distance, couldn't even lift his eyes, pounded his chest in shame, and prayed, "God, be merciful to me a sinner!" (Luke 18:13).

Which one do you think was on his way to closure for the sins of his past?

Joseph called his brothers spies, and they replied, "We are honest men" (Genesis 42:11).

If there was any word in any language that did not apply to these thugs, it's the word *honest*. Can you picture the first readers of this book laughing out loud? *Honest? Ha ha!*

Self-delusion isn't happiness.

Your happiness depends upon an ever-increasing alignment with reality. Call it spirituality. Call it maturity. Call it integrity. Whatever you call it, the *truth* will set you free.

Some people live with a festering shame for so long, they can no longer see what it does to them.

Thank God, he doesn't give up on them.

So there lay the brothers, facedown before this strange ruler, confused, panicked, conscience-stricken. Joseph repeated the charge of being spies.

At long last, something in them snapped. They took a first, faltering step toward truth. For the first time in the story, the brothers identified themselves by their relationship to Joseph—the *brother* who "is no more" (Genesis 42:13).

The truth was surfacing. Joseph was dragging their sorry behinds out of the quicksand of unreality. The brothers moved into a kind of limbo—a no-man's-land between reality and unreality.

I'm glad God allows for baby steps. I'm glad he loves us enough to bring us face-to-face with our unacknowledged chaos.

At this point, Joseph made an offer they couldn't refuse: Go home and fetch your youngest brother.

Why tell them that?

Because Joseph still couldn't trust them. Here they were, *claiming* a younger brother, but where was he? Why wasn't he with them? Joseph had to know if their hearts were changed.

"I'll just keep a hostage, while you fetch the little guy. Oh, and by the way, take three days to think about it. In prison."

Joseph knew from bitter experience the power of prison to concentrate the mind on things that matter most.

Just as Christ crucified spent three days in the grave, so the brothers spent three days in prison. They died a mini-death there, as Joseph had many years earlier. Death to old, familiar ways. Death to human-powered solutions. Death to unreality.

God loves you too much to subsidize your self-defeating ways forever.

He implanted a new life—supernatural and strong—deep in your soul. No matter how many barnacles have grown over it, it's there. Pulsing with energy. Radiating the happiness of God. Ready to express itself in faith, hope, and love. This life is in you already as God's child. It is who you are.

Let it shine.

Enough pretending to be something less. When Joseph locked his brothers in prison, he only made their outer circumstance match the inner truth they'd been living for twenty years: *They were already in prison and didn't know it.*

But now they did. Now there was no denying it.

They emerged on the third day with a new truth on their lips.

"We Are Truly Guilty"

Then they said to one another, "We are truly guilty concerning our brother, for we saw the anguish of his soul when he pleaded with us, and we would not hear; therefore this distress has come upon us." And Reuben answered them, saying, "Did I not speak to you, saying, 'Do not sin against the boy'; and you would not listen? Therefore behold, his blood is now required of us."

Genesis 42:21–22

Tolerating the intolerable for far too long, big brother Reuben boiled over. "We are truly guilty," he said.

He then asked the follow-up question every person conscious of their sins has dreaded: *Who will balance the scales of justice for me?*

Conscience never takes a vacation—and no matter how many therapists redefine sin as low self-esteem, there is something in the human heart crying out for justice.

Somebody has to pay.

The brothers felt it: "Now comes the reckoning for his blood" (Genesis 42:22 NASB).

Of all the teachings of theology, the single most self-evident, easily proven one is this: I am a sinner from a long line of sinners, and I need a Savior.

Jesus said, "Those who are well have no need of a physician, but those who are sick" (Matthew 9:12). If you want him to doctor your soul, you have to place yourself in the company of Joseph's brothers and others. Take full responsibility, quit buying your own false press, and come out of hiding.

By this, Jesus kisses "coping" good-bye. It's not about coping or therapy—though those things are good. He sees so much more. He sees total release, total healing, and total forgiveness for you.

After a nasty affair and a murder to cover it up, a king named David had a lot of unfinished guilt to take care of. He wrote:

> When I kept silent, my bones grew old
> Through my groaning all the day long.
> For day and night your hand was heavy upon me;
> My vitality was turned into the drought of summer.
> I acknowledged my sin to you,
> And my iniquity I have not hidden.

I said, "I will confess my transgressions to the LORD,"
And you forgave the iniquity of my sin.

Psalm 32:3–5

Back to Our Happy Place

Yes, we are still talking about a happy life.

The major premise is simple: The life God designed you to live is the happiest life of all. It radiates the joy of God (Nehemiah 8:10), and shares the happiness of Christ (John 17:13). This is the real you. Your true identity.

The minor premise is simple too: Anything less is unreality. You have entombed that spark of life beneath a mountain of crud. Whatever self-defeating labels or patterns exist in your life need to be brought to God and washed away.

Quit tolerating intolerable tolerations.

That's how you get closure.

When I fought becoming a pastor, I was fighting myself, resisting my own spiritual DNA. I buried that dream under a fear of what other people would think, under my own feelings of inadequacy and my terminal fears of failure.

I discovered I can't fight myself and not lose.

I am most happy when I am most myself.

May God bring you into that discovery ASAP. It took him some cajoling, but that's where he is about to bring Joseph's whole family.

<hr>

FOR REFLECTION AND DISCUSSION

1. List a handful of tolerations in your life. Which ones bother you the most?

2. Does your family tree keep secrets? Name some of them.

3. What effect do you think the brothers' twenty-year secret had on their lives? How would that play out in everyday life? In family gatherings?

4. What does God promise in 1 John 1:9?

5. What unfinished guilt or shame haunts you? Will you confess it to God? Will you make amends where you can?

Secret
#8

Identity

Unacquaintedness with our mercies, our privileges, is our sin as well as our trouble. . . . This makes us go heavily, when we might rejoice; and to be weak, where we might be strong in the Lord.[1]

—John Owen (1616–1683)

* * *

Know Your Riches

Know the riches of your new identity in grace,
because you are who God says you are no
matter what anyone else says.

* * *

I'd like to dig more into what I called the major premise in the previous chapter: *The life God designed you to live is the happiest life of all. It radiates the joy of God and shares the happiness of Christ. It is the real you. Your true identity.*

When I first started in ministry, I worked for a church that majored in children's ministry. I loved it. I was a young guy, full of energy and excited about serving God by serving children. Every day of the week our building crawled with kids like an urban tenement crawls with cockroaches. Fingerprints, scuff marks, breakage, chaos, the din of hordes of unruly youngsters echoing off cinderblock walls and concrete floors—it was a beautiful thing.

The heart and soul of our church was our tall, skinny, retired founding pastor named Lance B. Latham. We called him Doc. By the time I came on the scene, Doc was in his eighties and was retired. I knew him as a genius at organization, a virtuoso pianist, a gymnast, tennis player, and Scrabble lover. A wiry frame, a shock of white hair, and piercing eyes. Even into his eighties his grip was strong and his Scrabble skills unbeatable. I've already mentioned Doc Latham as one of my life's influencers.

The children's clubs he started in Chicago's "Roaring Twenties" spread around the globe as the Awana Youth Association.

In our church alone, tens of thousands of urban street kids encountered God and were set on a healthy path because of Doc's vision and love. With over 25,000 churches now using Awana worldwide, and over 1.5 million kids being cared for each week, the long shadow cast by this man is staggering.[2]

He also had a secret. He shared it over and over.

If you asked Doc Latham what's the most important thing to teach children, without hesitation he answered, "Teach them their riches in Christ."

That goes down as the best advice I've ever heard, not only for children, but for grown-ups too.

Three hundred fifty years ago, in his antiquated style, John Owen wrote, "Unacquaintedness with our mercies, our privileges, is our sin as well as our trouble." Translation: If you don't know your riches, you're messed up.

While most children's ministries major in *duty*—share, be kind, obey your parents, don't lie—Doc Latham majored in *identity*— who you are and what you have as God's child. That shift, from duty to identity, revolutionizes a life.

Like it did for Joseph's whole family. And like it did for me.

As Joseph's brothers received closure for the sins of the past, they needed something new to cling to. Like a smoker trying to quit, they needed not just to quit a bad habit, they needed to replace the bad habit with a new one. A healthy one.

It's the same for everybody. As we let go of past bad stuff, we need to seize future good stuff. But *what* future good stuff? *The good stuff of who you are and what you have because you belong to God.*

You need to lay hold of your true and deep identity in God and let it shine.

Grace Intervention

> Then Joseph gave a command to fill their sacks with grain, to restore every man's money to his sack, and to give them provisions for the journey. Thus he did for them.
>
> Genesis 42:25

No sooner had his brothers confessed their guilt, when Joseph began to secretly bless them.

The brothers still didn't know the true identity of this Egyptian ruler. Think what that meant. Their brother ran the show—they could bask in his glory if only they knew. But they didn't know, so they plastered their faces to the ground, groaning in dismay over what rats they were to Joseph long ago. They figured God was using the Egyptian to hammer them with justice.

Joseph, of course, understood their language. He turned away to cry. Why? Because he realized they *had* changed. They weren't the same men who abused him.

Still, they didn't totally come clean. There could be no redemption without that. So Joseph went to work. He deliberately set them in a new environment: the only one that creates freedom for moral train wrecks to spill their guts. Joseph showed them grace.

- He wept for them.
- He sold them grain.
- He secretly returned the purchase price of that grain.

- He supplied extra grain for their journey home.
- He ordered his royal servants to load their donkeys for them.

This same man, who not too long ago asked for grace (*hesed*) from the butler, didn't hesitate to show it to his brothers. He wanted them to be happy, but they weren't ready yet. So, like an ancient therapist, Joseph conducted history's first "grace intervention."

The brothers believed they were condemned, though they were forgiven.

They believed they were without rank, though they were sons of Israel (Prince with God) and brothers of Joseph (Ruler of Egypt).

They believed they were beggars, pleading for bread from a pagan monarch, though their sacks were filled with grain.

They didn't know their riches.

Know Your Riches

Knowing your riches dismantles your "kick me" past and reconstructs a new identity based on who God says you are.

You can always find people ready to label you according to your failures: you're stupid, ugly, too fat, too skinny, worthless, damaged goods, unwanted.

Even the devil joins the fray (Revelation 12:10).

What savage labels echo in the chambers of your mind? What names traumatized you and now dominate you?

God's whole plan intends to rehabilitate your massively dysfunctional view of self.

When you know your riches and embrace them, you stop letting anybody name you but God. You draw your identity from him, not from a harsh father, needy mother, dysfunctional peer group, cynical culture, or demeaning boss. Your losses, your defects, your wounds, and your victimhood no longer define you. God does.

The pilgrim-type Christians from three centuries ago called this "possessing your possessions." The idea was that you have this stuff, your name is on it, it belongs to you, so go use it.

Joseph's whole extended family was stuck in remedial class. They are about to get knocked upside the head into a long overdue promotion.

What Riches?

On the day you received Jesus, God deposited a portfolio of spiritual assets into your personal account in heaven. The Bible calls this your *inheritance*.[3] This portfolio adds up to a life-altering birthright.

Long before God flung the galaxies into space or filled the oceans with life, he looked down the corridors of time and previewed every day of your life. I've already mentioned how God saw every opportunity, every conflict, every relationship, every trial, every loss, every joy, and every test you will ever face. The Great Recession of 2008 didn't sneak up on him and shout "Boo!" God knew all your days before you were born.

But God didn't just *know*, he also *provided* for all your days. That's why David called him "my shepherd" and Abraham called him "The-Lord-Will-Provide."[4] I picture God wrapping mountains of dazzling gifts with exquisite bows and silver ribbons with my name inscribed on golden tags. The gifts contain supernatural resources for every moment of my life. Power. Wisdom. Friends. Laughter. Money. Food. Shelter. Creativity. Grace. Mercy. Peace. Courage. Pleasure. Meatballs. Tenderness. Love. All the stuff I crave and strive for and need. God has already deposited everything I need into my portfolio of spiritual assets. Past tense. Done. It's mine.

Now, he says, go take it. Unwrap the gifts.

(By the way, there's an expanded roster of your riches at the end of this chapter.)

Possess your possessions. Have you ever wondered why the Bible is called a new and old testament? Because it lists all the treasures in the inheritance Jesus unlocked for you by his death, like a last will and testament.

Sometimes I wonder why God should be this good to me. I haven't earned any Nobel prizes or made the world a measurably better place. So why me? Why should God lavish so much blessing on me?

Because of Whose You Are

A Christian is a person who has been superglued to Jesus. Bible experts call this a union with Christ. God united me with him when I first received him as my Savior. I am so united to Christ that everything that belongs to him now belongs to me. His treasures are my treasures. His inheritance is my inheritance. His resources are my resources.

I have been "blessed with every spiritual blessing" because I am one with Christ (Ephesians 1:3).

This is the heart of the Christian message.[5]

The essence of happiness is unwrapping God's treasures and using God's resources. You are rich beyond description in your possessions, and exalted to royalty in your status. This is reality for every child of God.

Happy yet?

If you look closely at my beautiful daughter's little finger, you'll find me wrapped tightly around it. One week, after church, she pestered me to buy expensive clothes for a fancy doll. I wasn't excited about doll clothing that costs as much as people clothing. In desperation, she dropped to her knees, folded her hands, smiled charmingly, and said, "Pleeeeeeazzzzze."

In public.

What's a daddy to do?

I told her, "Stand up. I'm your daddy; you don't have to beg."

God's children don't beg either.[6] God does not bless us because of our sincerity, intensity, or worthiness. He doesn't bless us because we read our Bible or prayed faithfully for three whole days straight.

He blesses us because of Jesus.

That's why we pray "in Jesus' name."

Besides, if we could earn our blessings, we'd have to call them "paychecks," not "blessings." But God gives them to us *gratis* because Jesus paid for them in full at the cross.

What if, every day, God invited us into our very own mini-Promised Land, lavished on us simply because of Jesus and prepared since the dawn of time? What if he invited us daily into a God-blessed life, even in the midst of a financially, politically, relationally, morally messed-up world?

Your riches in Christ prove once for all that your unhappiness has met its match.

To whatever degree you are unaware of these riches, you are like Joseph's clueless brothers.

Can You Say Irony?

Joseph loaded up the brothers with more treasures than they knew, and sent them home, without Simeon, to fetch little bro, Benjamin. The men returned home and told their father the mind-bending story. Then they unloaded their sacks only to find all their money had been returned.

Such grace fried their circuits. Their twisted hearts saw only a setup, a conspiracy to wipe them out. Father Jacob gushed out more drama than a teenage girl dumped just before homecoming.

> And Jacob their father said to them, "You have bereaved me: Joseph is no more, Simeon is no more, and you want to take Benjamin. All these things are against me."
>
> Genesis 42:36

Jacob spewed forth four laments, each one rooted in unreality:

1. Joseph is no more. (untrue)
2. Simeon is no more. (untrue)
3. And you would take Benjamin. (untrue)
4. All these things are against me. (untrue)

Every one of his complaints was backward. God had just made him rich beyond his wildest dreams; he was restoring his precious Joseph and raising his family to a place of dignity and love.

God was about to erase the mother of all tolerations in the aged patriarch's life. These things weren't *against* him, they were *for* him.

He was richer than he believed.

Don't make the same mistake. Get out of the remedial class, discover your riches, and embrace your identity.

Jacob doubted God's lavish goodness when it was staring him in the eye (abundant food in the midst of famine, and every penny returned).

The problem wasn't a deficit in God's supply, it was a gaping hole in Jacob's faith. Here was the son of Abraham and Isaac, a recipient of the magnificent promises of blessing, an heir of the riches of heaven, in the line of the Savior and of all who would believe—this great patriarch Jacob—living beneath his identity because he believed a lie.

Could it be that the lies you believe about God are killing your happiness day by day? That your suspicions against him are slaying your soul's satisfaction by the death of a thousand cuts? Could your thoughts of God be 180 degrees out of phase with reality?

The reality is this: God is for you. By his providence, he causes all things to work together for your good. By his grace, he loves you, protects you, empowers you, enjoys you, and cares for you day by day.

He has made you rich in things that money can't buy, and will care for you all your days.

All of this because of your perfect identity in Christ.

Even if you're an idiot.

Even if you fail again.

Even if the conspirators take over the country.

Even if the world stops spinning.

Even if anything.

Jacob suffered, not from a lack of grace, but from a culpable cluelessness of his true riches and identity.

Doc Latham was right. For anybody to preach sermons to Jacob about sharing, or not lying, or being a better person would have been a joke. He didn't need a message about *duty*, he needed to be reminded of his *identity*. He needed to remember who he was. He needed to embrace the single lesson God had been trying to beat into his head (literally, Genesis 32:24–28) for a lifetime: *You are my royal child, and my grace has supplied all you need. You are rich beyond measure, so quit acting like a moron.*

Jacob, out of fear, refused to let Benjamin return to Egypt with the brothers. "I'd rather starve," he said. So starve they did. Over there in Egypt, Jacob would find his long-lost son, Joseph, his newly lost son, Simeon, a royal welcome, and immeasurable blessing. And lots and lots of food.

Riches awaited, yet he loitered in the land of famine.

Just like I loitered in the land of "anything-but-pastor" for way too long. Just like so many loiter in the land of guilt, shame, self-loathing, and doubt. Or of loneliness. Or in that decaying swamp of revenge.

Riches are waiting.

Go get them.

The Famine That Won't Go Away

And may God Almighty give you mercy before the man, that he may release your other brother and Benjamin. If I am bereaved, I am bereaved!

Genesis 43:14

The famine deepened until Jacob gave in. "Fine," he said. "Take Benjamin and return to Egypt. If I am childless, so be it." I'm sure you remember the difference between true endurance and a grin-and-bear-it martyrdom. Jacob made himself die a thousand deaths before he ever died physically.

I wonder about myself sometimes: Why don't I live like spiritual royalty more often? Morning by morning, God lays an irresistible offer on the table. Why don't I take him up on it? Could it be I'm following the delinquent brothers and Jacob more than Joseph? That I squander more days than I realize, mesmerized by a distorted view of who I am?

You are an heir of the riches of Christ. Get that identity into your head, and a whole lot of Christian-type duties will flow out of you naturally.

Whatever else your inheritance includes, you can be sure it includes perfect provision for each day's need. Jesus inherits "all things," says the Bible, and you are a joint heir with him (Hebrews 1:2). Like Jesus, you are God's precious child, under his watchful care and sharing his royal status. That's who you really are. Not a cheater. You are not what any abuser, molester, exploiter, or loser says you are. You are not what your low self-esteem says you are. You are not what the bullies at school say you are. You are not what your financial advisor, or your ex, or your rap sheet says you are.

You are what God says you are, and he says you are united with Christ forever, sharing his identity, his riches, his status, and even his name. That's who you are.

Though your *behaviors* might paint a radically different picture, your identity is perfect because you belong to God. Any mismatch there is a problem you have to fix because it will kill your happiness.

Be who God made you to be.

Be yourself—your best self.

And quit calling yourself names; call yourself Christian. Take hold of your true nature as a redeemed, justified, beloved, adopted, forgiven, regenerated, blessed child of the King of Kings and Lord of Lords.

For years I heard a little voice in my head say, "You're stupid." Every time I made a mistake, it whispered, "You're stupid." I knew I wasn't stupid, but I couldn't make the voice shut up, so eventually it wore me down and I just thought I was stupid. It wasn't until I began listening to God's voice in his Word—hearing what God said about me—that a new sense of self came to life inside me.

Remember, you are most happy when you are most yourself.

The closure of the last chapter sets up the embrace of this chapter. Close the books on the sins of your past so you can embrace your glorious identity in the present and future.

You have two realities: the name God gives you and the name everybody else gives you. It's time to embrace your better reality.

And so the brothers trudged off to Egypt again, this time with the new youngest brother, Benjamin, in tow.

They are about to receive the shock of their lives.

Their brother is rich.

They are about to learn their riches in him.

Your Riches in Christ

The classic catalog of spiritual riches was compiled in the early 1900s by Lewis Sperry Chafer, the founder of Dallas Theological Seminary. He called it *The Riches of Grace in Christ Jesus* and included it in two of his books.[7] Since then the list has been updated, modified, and reprinted in many forms.

Chafer listed thirty-three riches, each with several sub-points, along with the Scripture references to support them all. I'm going to offer my own list, based on Chafer's, but formatted as a set of prayerful declarations. I hope you'll take the time to repeatedly and regularly pray through these riches and meditate on the Bible verses. Over time, your God-given identity will come to life inside you too.

Knowing these riches will shape you, will arm you for happiness in a cold, cruel world. Knowing these riches will free you from other people's craziness.

You will rise above a frantically grasping culture.

And you will increasingly become the real self you always dreamed you could be: deeply happy, by nature.

* * *

Who Am I?

1. I am united with Christ. (John 17:26; Galatians 2:20; 2 Corinthians 5:21)

2. I am crucified with Christ—so that his death counts for me. (Galatians 2:20; Romans 6:3, 6)

3. I am raised with Christ—so that his life can shine through me. (Romans 6:4–5, 11)

4. I am forgiven of all my sins. (Psalm 103:11–12; Ephesians 1:7; Colossians 1:14)

5. I am redeemed, set free from every force that holds me back. (Psalm 71:23; 1 Peter 1:18–19)

6. I am bought with a price, so I belong to God and he belongs to me. (1 Corinthians 6:20)

7. I am washed in the blood of Christ (*metaphorically speaking*). (Revelation 1:5; Isaiah 1:18)

8. I am complete in Christ. (Colossians 2:10)

9. I am a saint, holy in God's eyes. (1 Corinthians 6:11; Romans 1:7; 1 Corinthians 1:2)

10. I am guarded by the power of God. (1 Peter 1:5; 2 Corinthians 6:7; Romans 8:38–39)

11. I am born again, alive to God forever. (Titus 3:5)

12. I am a new creation with a new nature, new identity, new power, new destiny, and new name. (2 Corinthians 5:17)

13. I am spiritual royalty. (Revelation 1:6, 5:10; Ephesians 2:6)

14. I am a citizen of heaven. (Philippians 3:20)

15. I am free from condemnation. (Romans 8:1, 34)

16. I am justified, made perfect in God's sight forever. (Romans 5:1; Galatians 2:16; 1 Corinthians 6:11)

17. I am at peace with God. (Romans 5:1)

18. I am reconciled. (Colossians 1:21; 2 Corinthians 5:18)

19. I am robed in the righteousness of Christ. (Isaiah 61:10; Zechariah 3:3–5)

20. I am adopted. (Galatians 4:5; Romans 8:15)

21. I have access to God, immediate and everlasting. (Romans 5:2; Ephesians 2:18)

22. I am free. (John 8:32, 36; 2 Corinthians 3:17; Galatians 5:1)

23. I am an ambassador for Christ. (2 Corinthians 5:20; Ephesians 6:20)

24. I am God's soldier for grace, love, and truth. (2 Timothy 2:3; Ephesians 6:10–17)

25. I am empowered by God's own might. (Ephesians 6:10; Colossians 1:11)

26. I am the dwelling place of God—my heart is his home. (John 14:20; Romans 8:9; 1 Corinthians 2:11–12)

27. I am captain of my life, with dominion and a right to rule in my own sphere. (Romans 5:17)

28. I am able to do all things. (Philippians 4:13)

29. I am in the fellowship of the saints, the body of Christ, part of a worldwide family of faith. (Ephesians 2:19; Galatians 6:10; 2 Timothy 2:19)

30. I am accepted. (Ephesians 1:6; Luke 15:22–24)

31. I am always in God's care. (Romans 8:28; Matthew 6:30)

32. I am blessed. (Ephesians 1:3; Romans 8:32)

33. I am an heir of God and a joint-heir with Christ. (Romans 8:17)

34. I am loved. (John 3:16; Jeremiah 31:3; 1 John 4:10)

35. I am who I am by the grace of God. (1 Corinthians 15:10)

36. I am bound for heaven—a possessor of eternal life. (2 Corinthians 5:8; 1 John 5:11–12)

I am who God says I am. Nothing more. Nothing less.
This I believe through Christ, my Lord.
Amen.

For Reflection and Discussion

1. Have you ever found money you didn't know you had? What did you do with it?

2. How would you describe your self-concept? Your self-esteem?

3. How confident are you of the new identity God gave you when you met him through Christ?

4. What harmful labels from your past do you carry?

5. Is what God says about you really true? Are there voices in your head or your life speaking against God's truth?

6. According to 1 Corinthians 2:12, what "things" does God want you to know?

Secret
#9

Wisdom

Wisdom is heavenly discernment. It is insight into the heart
of things. Wisdom involves knowing God and the subtleties
of the human heart. More than knowledge, it is the right
application of knowledge in moral and spiritual matters, in
handling dilemmas, in negotiating complex relationships.[1]

—Oswald Sanders

* * *

Divine Viewpoint

View your life and adversities from heaven's perspective,
because your life's happiness is a subplot in
God's cosmic plan to bless the world.

* * *

As a boy growing up in the Midwest, the rules of baseball became
second nature to me by third grade. My dad played semi-pro
baseball on a farm team for the Chicago Cubs. He taught me
to catch with two hands, swing a bat level, and throw the ball
straight. He had me outside playing catch on lazy Sunday after-
noons. My friends and I rode our bikes to Oriole Park in Chicago

and played pickup games. Later, I joined Little League, though I was never very good. I understood balls and strikes, bunting and swinging away, fair balls and foul balls, tagging up and dropped third strikes. I never read a rule book, but I knew the rules.

Years later, as a doctoral student in California, I shared a room with a British pastor named James. I invited him to see the Angels play in Anaheim, and off we went. I watched as my dignified British friend dripped mustard down his chin while devouring his first hot dog.

The game began. James knew nothing about baseball. The pitcher wound up and delivered, high and outside. Ball one.

"What's that?" James asked.

"That's a ball."

"I know it's a ball. But what just happened?"

So I explained the strike zone and balls and strikes. He nodded like he understood.

The batter hit a ground ball for a single.

James asked, "Is that a point?"

"No," I said. "First of all, the *points* are called *runs*, and you don't get *runs* till he goes all the way home."

"Where?"

This led to a discussion of home plate, bases, base-running, scoring, outs, and innings.

The questions were endless.

After a while I gave up. "James, let's just enjoy the day."

He said, "One day, I'll take you to a cricket match."

I grinned. "Do they have hot dogs?"

"Bangers," he said.

"Forget it."

What was second nature to me—baseball and its complicated rules—was utterly alien to James. There was no way to cram a lifetime of knowledge into James' head within a single game.

In the beginning of this book, I offered Jeremiah Burroughs's classic statement: "Christian contentment is that sweet, inward, quiet, gracious frame of spirit, which freely submits to and delights in God's wise and fatherly disposal in every condition."

A happy life is, above all else, a "frame of spirit." It is an all-embracing way of looking at your life, a structure of belief and instinct that cannot be acquired by cramming.

When the umpire yells, "Play ball!" it's go time. No more practicing. When Joseph's brothers threw him in the pit, he had no time for Bible study, prayer meetings, or a crash course in overcoming adversity. What he had in his soul would have to do.

And what he had—his "frame of spirit"—was solid gold.

"I Am Joseph"

Then Joseph could not restrain himself before all those who stood by him, and he cried out, "Make everyone go out from me!" So no one stood with him while Joseph made himself known to his brothers. And he wept aloud, and the Egyptians and the house of Pharaoh heard it. Then Joseph said to his brothers, "I am Joseph; does my father still live?" But his brothers could not answer him, for they were dismayed in his presence. And Joseph said to his brothers, "Please come near to me." So they came near. Then he said: "I am Joseph your brother, whom you sold into Egypt."

Genesis 45:1–4

The author has drawn out the drama like an archer draws out a bow. When we thought we could take no more, he drew it farther. And now, finally, he lets it fly, and it's glorious.

Imagine that golden moment, when the petrified brothers heard the words, "I am Joseph."

I have to believe life shifted into slow-motion. They blanked out. They went numb.

I imagine furtive glances at one another. *Did you hear what I just heard? Did he say what I thought he said?*

Reality began to sink in. Joseph! The brother they hated. The one they threw into a pit and sold into slavery. This great ruler with all the power in the world is . . . Joseph?

What confusion!

But that's okay. Because confusion quickly gave way to sheer terror.

The brothers couldn't answer him. The Bible politely says, "For they were dismayed in his presence." The Hebrew word here refers to the terrifying "emotional disturbance" of someone who "is confronted with something unexpected, threatening, or disastrous."[2]

I'd say so. *What? We have been messing with Joseph?* What a bombshell! What a jolt!

And I love how the story goes. Joseph asked, "Is my father still alive?" And nobody could move. They were frozen in place.

So he invited them near and repeated himself, slowly, as if to children. "I am Joseph." This time he added, "Your brother . . . the one you sold into Egypt."

If ever you need a tangible picture of the love of God for guilty sinners, look no further than how Joseph embraced his brothers. What was in his soul?

Here comes the real gold. . . .

"God Sent Me"

> But now, do not therefore be grieved or angry with yourselves because you sold me here; for God sent me before you to preserve life. For these two years the famine has been in the land, and there are still five years in which there will be neither plowing nor harvesting.
>
> Genesis 45:5–6

"God sent me."

The brothers sold him, but God sent him.

That is a wisdom that comes only from above (James 3:17).

What would you have said to those brothers? What judgment day would you rain on their contemptible heads? Joseph was the second most powerful man in the most powerful nation on earth. He possessed godlike powers to punish, torture, and kill.

If ever, in the annals of history, there was a time for payback, Michael Corleone–style, this was it.

But not with Joseph. No hit man. No bloodshed. No hatred. No punishment. No bitterness. Nothing. "Do not be grieved or angry with yourselves," he said.

He completely let his guilty brothers off the hook.

Think about that.

I want to tread carefully here. Because, like Joseph, I'm sure you can point to people who wounded you. The last thing I want to suggest is that you make up some fiction and pretend that everything's okay when it's not okay.

That is not the point. We always have to deal with reality.

And Joseph did. He didn't varnish the facts of the case: *You sold me into Egypt,* he said. *You* did that. True.

But Joseph ran a clinic on yet another secret of a happy life: He interpreted his life from the perspective of heaven. It's as if he sat next to God and looked down on his life. He saw his losses. His joys. His dreams. His suffering. His dangers. His pain. His heartbreaks. His tears. His grief. His agony. His purpose. His strengths. His life's meaning. He saw all the dominoes from God's perspective.

Knowledge is a basic awareness of the facts, like reading baseball's rulebook.

Wisdom is having that knowledge integrated into your soul so that it is second nature, like instinctively knowing the rules of baseball and running the bases without thinking about it.

The difference between knowledge and wisdom is the difference between uninhibited dancing on the ballroom floor and counting steps in dance class—which is why I'm a terminal klutz, moves-wise.

Joseph thought God's thoughts after him. He had a lock on wisdom: "Happy is the man who finds wisdom, and the man who gains understanding" (Proverbs 3:13).

Through that wisdom he processed the events of a shattered life and reached the self-defining conclusion that *God* sent him there. From his time in the pit, through Mrs. Potiphar's lying accusation, through his days in prison and the butler's forgetfulness, God was running the whole show.

Wisdom produced in him a love of providence.

Joseph made peace with his tortured past on the basis of a divine perspective on life. Like few mortals, he personified Burroughs's definition: a "sweet, inward, quiet, gracious frame of spirit, which freely submits to and delights in God's wise and fatherly disposal in every condition."

News flash: You don't wake up one morning and exhibit such profound wisdom.

You grow into it.

You live your way into it, like a Chicago boy lives his way into the intricacies of baseball. Like a great chef lives her way into the nuances of *boeuf bourguignon*. Like my grandma could crochet the Eiffel Tower. It is not a choice as much as it is an all-encompassing frame of spirit. Not an action, but a mind-set. Not a surface level happiness, but a core happiness flowing from a heart that views life from God's chair.

Divine viewpoint thinking.

Wisdom.

What would God say about the journey of your life so far? What is his perception? His perspective? When he set up the dominoes that brought you to this place, what was he thinking? Which of his "wise and fatherly disposals" have you labeled blunders in the plan of God?

Your life is yours, but it is not only yours. Your life, above all else, belongs to God. You exist for his purposes. You will either rest your heart within this truth, or spend all your days as a victim of a God you've transmogrified into a cosmic schoolyard bully.

God's purposes are bigger than your purposes, and he has every right to deploy you as he sees fit. Your identity equips you for this deployment. God crafted a perfect match between your identity and his purposes for your life.

Don't worry, his purposes sizzle with beauties to overflow the finite mind with joy beyond your wildest dreams. C. S. Lewis wrote:

> We are half-hearted creatures, fooling about with drink and sex and ambition when infinite joy is offered us, like an ignorant

child who wants to go on making mud pies in a slum because he cannot imagine what is meant by the offer of a holiday at the sea. We are far too easily pleased.[3]

Infinite joy. That's God's purpose.
Sounds good to me.

To Preserve Life

Joseph said, "God sent me here."

Wait a minute. Who sent him to Egypt? His brothers, right? Right. So how can he say God sent him?

He could say that because his years of solitude in prison and in slavery—his years of sitting alone in the throne room because the Egyptians wouldn't keep company with a Jew—forced him into communion with God. God was his community. God was his companion, his company, and his friend.

The stronger that bond became, the more it dawned on him that if God was truly on his side, Joseph was nobody's victim.

And neither are you.

Let that sink in.

When those brothers sold Joseph into slavery, God concurred. *So did Joseph.* That's why he never went back home: He embraced the grand purpose hiding behind the veil of his sorrows.

Did that make God guilty of evil? No. The brothers did the evil, not God. God cannot, will not, and has not done evil, nor has he tempted anybody to do evil (James 1:13; Habakkuk 1:13).

God permits evil to run its course, like a homeowner permits a rabid rodent to take solid hold of the cheese.

Then he springs the trap.

The other day, my son's football coach, Mike, asked me why God lets evil people get away with it. I asked him, "How would you like to live in a universe where God stamps out evil as soon as it happens?"

He smiled and said, "No thanks."

If God were to stamp out all evil when it occurred, the world would be a mighty lonely place. Do not doubt, however, his foot is lifted and the gargantuan stomp of justice is coming.

But God is giving evildoers—like me and you—time to get out of the way.

No evil gets overlooked in the coming judgment day of God.

God is not the author of evil. Evil galloped into the world through free-will agents like Adam, Eve, and the devil. And me and you. Suffering and death came riding in on evil's back. Though God doesn't cause evil, he can and does hijack it to bring about a greater good.

That greater good is mind-blowing.

> And God sent me before you to preserve a posterity for you in the earth, and to save your lives by a great deliverance. So now it was not you who sent me here, but God; and he has made me a father to Pharaoh, and lord of all his house, and a ruler throughout all the land of Egypt.
>
> Genesis 45:7–8

Who were these brothers that Joseph saved?

They were the bloodline of the world's Savior. They were bearers on earth of God's promised salvation.

They faced two fatal dangers and never realized it.

First, they faced the danger of assimilating with the evil culture around them (remember Genesis 38 with Judah, Tamar, and Onan?). There was a genuine danger that, through intermarriage and religious compromise, the physical and spiritual bloodline of the Savior would puff out like a candle.

The second fatal danger was that their race would not survive the coming famine that swept the known world—that the line of the Savior would go *poof!*

So God, in his providence, implemented a master plan. He strategically positioned Joseph, in that place, at that time, to preserve the remnant of the Jews and with them, to preserve people from every tongue, tribe, and nation for all eternity.

By choosing Egypt, God chose the one major nation on earth that wouldn't intermingle with the Jews (Genesis 43:32). The Jews would keep their faith in God intact and their bloodline pure.

All this burst on Joseph's mind like a fireworks finale. He interpreted his entire torturous journey from the divine perspective. He didn't see himself as a victim of evil men, or of blind luck, or of mindless fate. He was nobody's victim. He didn't define himself by the losses of his past, but rather by God's promise for his future.

By choice, he kissed misery good-bye and seized a happiness no one could take away.

When you integrate divine wisdom into your consciousness, you become increasingly immune to other people's craziness. You see yourself as nobody's victim.

If you could fly a spaceship to heaven, spend fifteen minutes with God, observe him ordering the universe, commanding the angels, paying attention to the pickiest details of your life, and then, if you could fly back to planet earth to live out your days, would that change you? Would you ever wring your hands again? Would you fear? Whine? Pout?

No.

To see as God sees is the pinnacle of happiness.

When you finally see your twisted tale from heaven's omniscient perspective, you will clap your hands and say, "I wouldn't change a thing."

Back to the Brothers

In one minute the brothers' lives have been turned topsy-turvy. *Joseph isn't dead! He is alive! He is ruler of all Egypt! We are bowing before him, just as his dreams foretold.*

What a shock to the system! For twenty-two years, these men carried a secret shame they did not need to carry. They lived in unreality.

That is exactly the point of this chapter. You will either see your life from a fallen human perspective, or from a glorious divine perspective.

One is unreality.

What if you have spent a lifetime learning the wrong rules to the game? Where did you get your ideas about happiness, anyway? Odds are strong you *absorbed* them from parents, peers, and the culture all around you. Like a kid absorbs how to season the spaghetti sauce from an Italian grandmother, you absorbed the rules of happiness from whatever environment you grew up in.

There's a fatal flaw in that system: Its rulemakers suffer a defect. "All have sinned," the Bible says, "and fall short of the glory of God" (Romans 3:23). We are fallen members of a fallen race. Don't take that personally—it's universal. The natural mind, unaided by the wisdom of God, screws it up every time (1 Corinthians 2:14). Our culture's rules of happiness have been crafted by morally corrupt, emotionally dysfunctional, and mentally blinded rulemakers. By the Mrs. Potiphars and the Joseph's Brothers of the world.

They pursued happiness in their own way, and by their own rules. Enough said.

What you've absorbed is flawed.

It's time to ingrain new rules. Enter: the Bible.

Time to pick up the bat, step up to God's plate, and take a few swings. It might feel awkward, but everybody starts somewhere. Make the Bible your daily companion. Attend a church with good Bible teaching, and then don't skip weekends. Absorb God's truths. Like a musician practicing your scales till you can do them with your eyes closed, make the promises, commandments, truths, doctrines, and principles of God's Word your second nature.

Jesus, quoting Moses, declared, "Man shall not live by bread alone, but by every word that proceeds from the mouth of God" (Matthew 4:4). And wise King Solomon advised:

> Get wisdom! Get understanding! Do not forget, nor turn away from the words of my mouth. Do not forsake her, and she will preserve you; love her, and she will keep you. Wisdom is the principal thing; therefore get wisdom. And in all your getting, get understanding. Exalt her, and she will promote you; she will bring you honor, when you embrace her. She will place

on your head an ornament of grace; a crown of glory she will deliver to you.

Proverbs 4:5–9

Sounds like a recipe for deep happiness.

With divine viewpoint filling your heart, you will see your life as Jesus saw his life. A friend in need will call you, and you will love like Jesus loved. A big fat adversity will drop into your lap, and you will react like Jesus would react. You're both cooking from the same recipes.

That's why Jesus promised, "These things I have spoken to you, that my joy may remain in you, and that your joy may be full" (John 15:11).

What things has he spoken? Divine wisdom from above. The whole Bible.

For my friend James, baseball was a mystery. He hadn't read the book and he hadn't played the game.

Read the Book. Live the Book.

Bigger Than You Realize

A while back, my church offered a special service for long-married couples to renew their wedding vows. As the day drew close, our team worked hard to make the day special. We gave our regular worship team the day off and hired a string quartet. We rented tuxes for our pastoral team. We set up gorgeous floral arrangements, hung bunting from the rafters, installed special lighting, stripped the stage of all extraneous gear, and placed a white runner down the center aisle. We made everything as classy and as elegant as we could.

It was beautiful.

When the big day came, our couples arrived to a transformed church. They were blown away.

With tears in her eyes, one of the brides said, "Bill, this is so beautiful! Thank you so much. If I had only known what a big thing this was, I would have dressed nicer."

God has written a story. It arcs from his pre-creation solitude to the acclamation of ten thousand times ten thousand ransomed beings in the new heaven and new earth. Within that story you'll find enough drama to energize a teenage daughter's text messaging for a millennium. Each of us lives, dies, and lives again as interconnected subplots in God's grand story. From our perspective on this anthill called earth, the story unfolds one nerve-wracking line at a time. But from God's perspective on Mount Eternity, the story has already been written to a breathtakingly satisfying conclusion.

Right now you see your life as through a microscope. Your own issues fill your horizon.

One day you will see how everything that happened to you was part of a much larger story. How your experiences—good and bad—contributed to God's cosmic plan for the ages.

When that happens you will say, "If only I had known what a big thing this was, I would have dressed nicer."

As you build up biblical wisdom in your soul, God grants you a backstage pass to that bigger picture today. He hints at a coming fireworks display to dazzle the angels for eternity, and then shoots off periodic samples to keep you motivated. He promises to make up for the bad times better than you can dream, and drops some unexpected blessings on your doorstep to keep you encouraged. He offers guidance for moral dilemmas, encouragements for emotional trials, strength for physical demands, and understanding for the logical challenges you face every day. God intends for you to build his wisdom into your *psyche* today that you might celebrate the happily-ever-after long before you see it happen.

"Tell My Father"

So you shall tell my father of all my glory in Egypt, and of all that you have seen; and you shall hurry and bring my father down here.

Genesis 45:13

150

"Dad," I said. "Are you proud of me?"

I was twenty-something. I knew my gruff old Italian dad loved me; he proved it ten thousand different ways. But I couldn't remember hearing him say he was proud of me. So I asked him. I had worked my way through college, was working as a young minister, and was living on my own.

"Are you proud of me?" I asked.

"I've always been proud of you, son," he responded.

Manly hug.

He's in heaven now, but that conversation was one of my life's happiest moments. Every kid longs for Dad's approval.

"Tell my father of all my glory," said Joseph.

I get you, buddy.

What if you don't have a dad? What if he's too self-absorbed to notice you? What if he's so twisted you don't want his approval?

Good news: You have another Father. He's cheering you on. He's on your side. He's for you, not against you. He's your craziest fan.

Your happiness is always on his mind.

When you persistently grow in wisdom—when you build God's biblical perspective into your thoughts, beliefs, and instincts—you stand in line for two glorious rewards:

Your Father in heaven will be proud of you.

Your joy will be full.

FOR REFLECTION AND DISCUSSION

1. What complicated things are you good at? Cooking, sports, mathematics, dancing—what have you done so often for so long that it's second nature for you?

2. Is God's truth that familiar to you? Can you see how wisdom would promote your happiness?

3. Have you or has someone you know gone through trials that made no sense until after the fact?

4. In general, how well do you react to difficulty? What does this say about you?

5. How did Joseph's suffering contribute to God's cosmic plan for the universe?

6. What problem does the Bible address in 1 Corinthians 3:1–2?

Secret
10

Surrender

The adventures may be mad, but the adventurer must be sane.
—G. K. Chesterton

* * *

Respect for the "Godness" of God
Quit pushing back against God's ways, because he is
working for your joy, even when you don't see it.

* * *

"Okay, Coach"

Though I know little about the technical side of football, I know
enough to help coach my son's Junior Pee Wee team. My chief con-
tribution is helmet-snapping—crucial for a team of nine-year-olds.

At that age, kids have a tendency to lose focus, make excuses, and
bicker—especially when the weather is hot and the hitting is hard.

They also talk back to our head coach, Mike—a big no-no
as far as Coach Mike is concerned. I am teaching one player in
particular to stick with two responses: "Yes, Coach" and "Sorry,
Coach." I promised his life will be easier if he sticks with that.

But no, he has to talk back.

Coach Mike yells, "Jimmy, how come you didn't block that guy?"

Jimmy replies, "Tommy pushed me and my finger hurts and the sun—"

"That's enough," Coach Mike says. "Take a lap!"

Too bad. If only he had stuck with, "Sorry, Coach." The coach is the coach. Button your lip. Do your job. Hit hard. No excuses.

Sometimes I think God would love to hear a simple, "Yes, God" or "Sorry, God" without a litany of excuses, resentments, suggestions, corrections, rationalizations, and denials.

Search Joseph's tale from beginning to end, and you'll find not a syllable of pushback against God or the plays he called. Whatever God brought to the table, Joseph ate, no complaints.

As we've seen, you can't break God's laws. You can't spoil his plan. You can only break yourself against God's plan.

If you're playing tug-of-war with God, I have a suggestion.

Surrender. Quit pushing back against God's ways, because he is working for your joy, even when you don't see it.

Let's play the Joseph story at triple speed: After whipping off his ruler-mask and revealing his secret identity to his brothers, he sent them home to fetch Dad back to Egypt. Dad wept for joy, kissed famine good-bye, and danced all the way to the new land of plenty.

What a reunion! Joseph's aged father, Jacob, wept with joy at the sight of his long-lost son. More manly hugs. Joseph's whole family moved to Egypt and lived happily ever after, for a very long time. The sons of Jacob, aka Israel, were truly blessed.

One of Joseph's capstone lessons on happiness came from a mysterious incident just before Father Jacob died.

The Blessing

Now the eyes of Israel [Jacob] were dim with age, so that he could not see. Then Joseph brought [his sons] near him, and he kissed them and embraced them. And Israel said to Joseph, "I had not thought to see your face; but in fact, God has also shown me your offspring!" So Joseph brought them from beside his knees, and he bowed down with his face to the earth. And Joseph took them both, Ephraim with his right hand toward Israel's left hand, and Manasseh with his left hand toward Israel's right hand, and brought them near him.

Genesis 48:10–13

Jacob tottered in as a spunky centenarian; he would soon die a happy man.

The time had come for Jacob to give his blessing to Joseph's strapping Egypt-born sons.

This blessing was like a prayer on steroids. It served up a legally binding, spiritually critical last will and testament.

Joseph arranged his sons in just the right place opposite half-blind Jacob. That's because Joseph's firstborn, Manasseh, stood in line for Jacob's double blessing. Manasseh's privileged position was sealed by Jacob's *right* hand landing on his head and Jacob's *left* hand on Ephraim's head.

So Joseph placed Manasseh opposite Jacob's right hand, and Ephraim opposite Jacob's left hand. In typical Joseph fashion, everything was decent and in order until something went weirdly wrong.

Once again, God blew down the dominoes in the wrong direction.

Then Israel [Jacob] stretched out his right hand and laid it on Ephraim's head, who was the younger, and his left hand on Manasseh's head, guiding his hands knowingly, for Manasseh was the firstborn.

Genesis 48:14

Jacob crossed his arms and planted his gnarled knuckles on the opposite heads. Was this senility rearing its ugly head? Or was something deeper going on?

This is beautiful.

By *rights*, the older son should have received the birthright. But by a sovereign decision of *grace*, the younger son—the son without rights or privilege—received it.

Cagey old Jacob knew exactly what he was doing: He was giving his family a permanent object lesson on grace. He finally got it, and he wanted every generation downstream to get it too.

Jacob crossed his arms and placed his hands on the two young men's heads. Then he spoke the blessing.

The Blessing

And he blessed Joseph, and said: "God, before whom my fathers Abraham and Isaac walked, the God who has fed me [literally "shepherded me"] all my life long to this day, the Angel who has redeemed me from all evil, bless the lads; let my name be named upon them, and the name of my fathers Abraham and Isaac; and let them grow into a multitude in the midst of the earth."

Genesis 48:15–16

There's a subtle but crucial lesson tucked in here to save us a lot of grief on our quest for happiness. Jacob learned this lesson late in life; he would have spared himself loads of needless drama had he embraced it earlier.

The lesson flows out of what Jacob says here about God.

1. "God has been my shepherd all my life."
2. "God has been my Angel who has kept me from all harm."

Really, Jacob? What about all the tragedies, the losses, and the pain? What about burying your sweet wife, Rachel? And losing Joseph for all those years? What about your sons' deception? What about the famine? Your life has been an emotional roller coaster, yet you proclaim God as your shepherd and protector.

Just one chapter earlier, when Jacob stood before Pharaoh and was asked his age, Jacob said, "The days of the years of my pilgrimage *are* one hundred and thirty years; few and evil have been the days of the years of my life" (Genesis 47:9).

In chapter 47, Jacob said, "I've had a wretched, miserable life."

In chapter 48, he said, "God has been my shepherd all my life and has kept me from all harm."

What changed?

For the first time in his soap opera saga, Jacob discovered what his son Joseph discovered as a teenager: *Jacob discovered a respect for the "Godness" of God.* He came to terms with his role as "the clay" and God's role as "the Potter."

A kissing cousin of this truth says that what makes life hard is not God's work of molding the clay to his own specifications, but the clay fighting back.

Surrender.

Over a millennium later, God would tell Saul of Tarsus, "It is hard for you to kick against the goads" (Acts 9:5). Goads, prods, spurs—whatever you call them—the Master and Commander of the cosmos has ways to stimulate action in the direction he desires.

For Saul, God pulled out his heavenly cudgel and whacked him upside the head, knocking him right off his horse (Acts 9:1–9). Saul stopped kicking—and became a happy champion of the grace of God.

For Jacob, God used a gentler approach: He gave him back his son. Jacob's lifetime of fighting, scrapping, wrestling, and conniving his way to happiness evaporated. When he reconsidered the torturous twists and turns of his life, Jacob, for this first time in his drawn-out tale, saw God had been there all along.

What will it take for God to make you stop kicking against his ways?

There's the hard way and the less hard way. Sorry, but there's no easy way.

The hard way is to keep getting ticked off at God.

The less hard way is to accept his ways as best.

So Jacob called on this God who was his shepherd—this God who kept him from all harm—and asked him to bless his grandsons.

But there was still that funky problem where Jacob had his hands on the wrong heads. Joseph objected.

> Now when Joseph saw that his father laid his right hand on the head of Ephraim, it displeased him; so he took hold of his father's hand to remove it from Ephraim's head to Manasseh's head. And Joseph said to his father, "Not so, my father, for this one is the firstborn; put your right hand on his head." But his father refused and said, "I know, my son, I know. He also shall become a people, and he also shall be great; but truly his younger brother shall be greater than he, and his descendants shall become a multitude of nations." So he blessed them that day, saying, "By you Israel will bless, saying, 'May God make you as Ephraim and as Manasseh!'" And thus he set Ephraim before Manasseh.
>
> Genesis 48:17–20

I love what happened here: Joseph argued with his dad. That makes me feel right at home. Nothing presses your buttons like a visit from your old mom or dad.

"No, Dad, I had the kids in the right place. Right hand here, left hand there. Sheesh!" Joseph reached out and grabbed his father's arm.

Jacob wouldn't let him.

"I know, I know," Jacob said, shrugging off Joseph's hand. "I know what I'm doing. They are both blessed, but the second-born is more blessed. The one without rights. The younger brother obtains the blessing of which he is unworthy. Get it?"

"Okay, Dad"

Joseph argued with his father's will. But his father stood firm. There was no real explanation. No good reason. Just a richly unsatisfying rebuff: "I know what I'm doing."

And that was enough for Joseph. He completely backed down.

"Okay, Dad."

Fundamental fact of life: *What God has in mind is always better than what you and I have in mind.*

How many times have you corrected your heavenly Father? And how many times has he told you, "I know what I'm doing"?

Then how many times have you come back with, "No, you don't." Before you know it, you're lifting his hand and challenging him to an arm wrestle. Your life with him devolves into a big fat fight, and he gets nothing from you but the cold shoulder.

An old friend lost her business and won't forgive God.

A fellow pastor lost his ministry and hasn't prayed since.

A lifetime friend lost her marriage and blamed God more than her swine of a husband.

"God, you're wrecking my life," you say.

"I know what I'm doing," he says.

"No, you don't. You have to do it this way . . ." And you lift his hand.

So another layer of hardness grows on an increasingly calloused heart.

When Margi and I lost our first baby to miscarriage, I couldn't pray for weeks. I had to press through till I could say, "Yes, God." I still don't understand it. Dominoes. Somehow. Surrender.

Years later, when my son needed surgery, it was difficult to sing God's praise. I made myself do it. "Yes, God."

When I encountered a time of brutally needless drama—from Christians—I lost all desire to seek wisdom from God's Word. I read my Bible anyway, by force of will. "Yes, God."

The greatest danger of an argument with God is that you will let the conflict fester; that you will reopen the scab at every turn, letting bitterness, like a swarm of flies, consume your respect for him.

Take a lesson from Joseph: He argued once and then shut up. Even though his Inner Lawyer could easily make a winning case against Jacob's crossed arms, Joseph acquiesced to his father's will.

He acquiesced to God's will too.

In fact, he loved God's will. For Joseph, God's strange turns— even the painful ones—delivered to him the life of his dreams.

With all his power, wealth, money, and fame he would have beat a hasty path right back to the Promised Land if his new land had not felt like home.

You can't fight God and feel happy.

What about you? What unplanned interruptions detour your plans? What painful losses make you question the divine? When every rational molecule in your being demands God to uncross his inexplicably crossed hands, what will you do?

Here's my advice: When you see God going south when you're convinced he should go north, go ahead and complain. Tell him. Talk to him about it. Correct him. Lay all your suggestions on his table. Give him your complaints. Do your level best to lift his hand.

I really mean it. Go ahead and advise God how to be God.

Once. Twice. Three times at the most (2 Corinthians 12:7–9).

Get it out of your system.

Then be quiet and enjoy the ride.

"Okay, Dad."

Consider life's twists and turns as Jeremiah Burroughs described: golden opportunities to "freely submit to and delight in God's wise and fatherly disposal in every condition."

Don't turn bitter.

Don't feel sorry for yourself.

Don't be a victim.

Don't play the martyr.

Don't lash out.

Don't isolate yourself.

Don't cross that line you know you shouldn't.

Don't throw away your Bible.

Don't quit church, faith, worship, or hanging out with God's people.

"Father, I don't get it, but I trust you. You've got better things in mind for me than I can imagine. You do all things well. Especially dominoes."

Surrender. Submit to and delight in God's twists and turns. Your life will be so much easier. God promises.

The Death of Jacob

After years in Egypt, Jacob went the way of all flesh and met his Maker. In a tragic coda to the story, Joseph's brothers again freaked out. You wonder, *What's it going to take for God to get anything through their Neanderthal skulls?* They said, "Now that Dad's dead, Joseph will come gunning for us."

Why can't they wrap their pea-brains around the wonder of grace?

Here are Joseph's final recorded words to these redeemed delinquents:

> Joseph said to them, "Do not be afraid, for am I in the place of God? But as for you, you meant evil against me; but God meant it for good, in order to bring it about as it is this day, to save many people alive."
>
> Genesis 50:19–20

God is on his throne. God rules. His providence shepherds even the most random details of your life to their awe-inspiring ends.

Would you go through hell and back if you knew your troubles would save hundreds of thousands of people from starvation (including your family), and deliver countless thousands into an encounter with the living God (including your family), bringing them to heaven forever, while simultaneously elevating you to the most powerful, wealthiest throne on earth?

"Am I in the place of God?" Joseph asked. No. Of course not. Are you?

On your good days, you know the answer.

No offense intended, but I'm glad you're not God.

And you should be glad I'm not God. Even I am glad I'm not God.

Because only God's ways are ways of grace. If you or I were God, heaven would be empty, because we would reserve it for life's well-deserving firstborn—life's upstanding moral high achievers. No one would measure up.

If you or I were God, we would fry Joseph's brothers in hell's skillet forever.

So Jacob crossed his arms and wove grace for the unqualified into the fabric of God's forever family.

And Joseph crossed his arms and blessed his hoodlum brothers.

And God nailed his Son's arms to a cross on Mount Calvary. So the morally undeserving second-borns of earth are welcomed into the blessings of heaven.

As unworthy as you might feel, when you walk with God, he offers joy beyond measure and mercies packed in so tightly you can't cram any more in.

He promised abundance (John 10:10). He promised peace (John 14:27). He promised riches money can't buy (Matthew 6:20). He promised joy (John 17:13).

He is taking you to a deeply happy life within a deeply happy universe.

Surrender.

Submit.

Admit that a good deal of your misery flows out of a resentment against God. Let it go. Humble yourself under his mighty hand.

And if you must, go ahead and correct God. But then be quiet. Respect the Godness of God. Accept his ways. Embrace him as a good and gracious God, the shepherd of your soul, and the One who, in his brilliantly meandering way, still makes dreams come true. I promise you a happy life if you do.

"Okay, God."

<hr>

FOR REFLECTION AND DISCUSSION

1. Have you or has someone you loved ever tried to correct God? Name a couple of those situations. How did they turn out?

2. When Jacob crossed his arms for the blessing of Joseph's sons, Joseph was puzzled and perhaps exasperated. What unusual events in your life would fall into the same category?

3. Do you know anyone pushing back against God for the twists and turns of providence? How is that working for them? What advice might you give?

4. When was the last time you said "Okay, God" in a time of adversity? Is this something you might want to do more often?

5. What does St. Paul's experience in 2 Corinthians 12:7–9 reveal about a heart that respects the Godness of God?

======= Love =======

There is no other life, like that of love. Nothing brings us so much happiness—as living for others, giving out our lives in sweet helpfulness, whatever the cost may be. The sweetest happiness which we can get in the world, comes from adding a little to the happiness of others.

—J. R. Miller

* * *

A Transcendent Cause

Donate your life to loving purposes, because anyone who wants to find a happy life must lose it first.

* * *

What if the deepest secret of a happy life was to seek happiness for others, even at the expense of yourself?

Joseph might have some experience with that. He was a one-man life-improvement machine.

- Jacob's life was better—Joseph was his favorite son for good reason.
- Potiphar's life was better—Joseph managed his entire household meticulously.

- Mrs. Potiphar's life was better, though she refused to be satisfied.
- The prison warden's and the butler's lives were better, though I speculate the baker didn't much like Joseph.
- Pharaoh's life was better.
- Jacob's family's lives were better.
- The land of Egypt avoided mass starvation and famine.
- All the nations who came for food fared better because of Joseph.

Joseph sacrificed. Others benefited. In this way, he was a forerunner of Jesus.

When Jesus set his face toward death, you might think a cloud of depression shrouded his view. Yet according to Scripture, he marched forward "for the joy that was set before Him" (Hebrews 12:2). Joy? What joy?

His joy at overcoming his own adversity.

His joy over a fallen race set free by his great sacrifice on Calvary's cross.

His joy over crushing the head of evil and sealing Satan's doom by his resurrection.

His joy at a coming celestial party to end all parties, an explosion of happiness from saints and angels and God who does all things well.

Jesus saw all that happiness ahead and pressed through the agonies of his crucifixion.

For the *joy* set before him. "Joy to the world, the Lord is come."

Jesus found his happiness in creating our happiness, just like Joseph and hosts of others who've followed their steps.

You picked up a book about a happy life. I have offered no tricks, no shortcuts, no gimmicks.

Just one man's story opening a window to the heart of a God whose hearty laughter shakes creation's foundations.

I'm writing this chapter on the heels of a string of airline nightmare experiences. While flying to a speaking engagement, our plane took off, flew half an hour, turned around and landed where we started. Fire trucks circled our aircraft as the pilot told us to "sit tight" while they checked for fuel leaks.

Right.

We pulled up to the gate and deboarded. "Take all your belongings with you, but remain near the gate."

Check.

Three and a half bewildering hours later, we were airborne again.

As we reboarded, a sweaty, glistening man behind me in the Jetway stood muttering and fuming. "So many hours late!" he said. He cursed. He stamped his foot. He cursed again. His face was red, and the little vein on his temple looked ready to pop. A grown-up hissy fit. I looked around at our fellow passengers. No doubt we all had airline horror stories to share.

But in that line, on that day, only one man made himself miserable, and he had no qualms about sharing the misery with everyone in earshot. What a sweetheart!

I was not feeling the love.

When life crashes on your head and you can still love your neighbor, you've got magic going on.

You can't opt out of adversity, but you can opt out of misery. This is not easy, and it takes ever-increasing faith, which itself takes ever-increasing maturity.

The Spiritual Baby

In the Bible's famous "Love Chapter," St. Paul offers a series of contrasts between the love of an immature person and a mature person. He writes, "For now we see in a mirror, dimly, but then face to face . . ." (1 Corinthians 13:12). President Kennedy's challenge to our nation to put a man on the moon paled in comparison to a sky-high challenge from Paul.

A childish person, the Bible says, "sees in a mirror, dimly."

Question: When you're looking in a mirror, who are you looking at?

Answer: yourself.

More to the point, are you gazing at your own needs, your own problems, your own woes, your own wounds? The smell of narcissism rises off an immature person like the wavy lines of stink from a cartoon skunk. If you live for you and yours, never venturing outside your own skin long enough to invest in a world in need, you're an "I-guy" (or I-gal), as Coach Mike says.

Not only do you see all of life in a mirror, but you do so "dimly." The original Greek word here gives us our English word, *enigmatically*. Narcissism makes life a riddle. When you live for yourself, life makes no sense. Your own fat face gets in the way of your sense of purpose, your self-worth, and ultimately, your happiness.

You may overflow with power, wealth, fame, status, beauty, and popularity. You may drip with degrees and letters above your peers. You may beautify yourself with surgeries, drape your body in designer fashions, adorn your home with soothing *fêng shui,* and dress your kids in Nordstrom's finest. You might even help serve coffee in the church foyer on Sunday and sing on the worship team once a month.

To the degree that you're doing it for "me, myself, and I," you are stuck in spiritual kindergarten. You are spiritually immature. You are bowing before the mirror of self-love and baffled by the enigma of how so much stuff can bring so little happiness.

You need to grow up in God.

You need to break orbit with yourself so you can orbit God and the world he loves so passionately.

The Spiritual Champion

On the flip side of the spiritual baby, the spiritual champion ditches the mirror and sees "face to face." Like Joseph, you see beyond your own needs enough to lend a hand to others, helping them climb up from the wreckage of morally depraved lives.

In her journal, Helen Keller wrote, "Many persons have a wrong idea of what constitutes true happiness. It is not attained through self-gratification but through fidelity to a worthy purpose."

"When I became a mature person, I put away childish things," said Paul.

A transcendent cause.

Egypt gave Joseph a purpose bigger than himself, something worth living and dying for. He donated his life to bless, to serve, to help, to elevate the people of Egypt, even at great personal cost.

Love is self-sacrifice to meet another's need.

Behind the sacrifice he found joy. He was willing to pay the price of permanent exile if it meant the happiness of saving lives and honoring God before a profoundly messed-up world.

Joseph loved God. He loved the Egyptian people. He loved a starving world. He loved his family. He loved outside his own tight circle. He loved the brothers who disowned him. He loved his enemies.

He lived and died for a noble cause beyond himself.

He was a spiritual champion, a hero of grace. And he was a happy man.

Joseph's story could have ended very differently. If anyone ever had an excuse to "take care of number one," it was Joseph. His early life was littered with trauma, cruelty, suffering, and loss.

Yet he triumphed in the end through love, the ultimate and final secret of happiness.

We all have seasons of difficulty when we must tend to our own needs and take care of ourselves. That's legit, but it is not to be the total story of our lives. Love your family well—or, if you don't have a family, create a new community for yourself at church or in your circle of friends. Be loyal to your own circle, but don't stop there.

Transcend your "me first" instincts. Teach your whole family or circle of friends to ditch the mirror. Be the catalyst.

Volunteer at church or at your kids' school. Give financially to worthy causes. Hammer nails with Habitat for Humanity. Serve meals to homeless people on holidays. Open your eyes to the people around you, your heart to the hurts around you, and your wallet to the needs around you.

Make love your way of life.

Happiness needs love like lasagna needs cheese.

Love fuels happiness, not the other way around.

Ready for Love?

But love takes maturity.

When I was a boy, our church told a story so beautiful it sounded like an urban legend, but it was really true. The church kitchen needed new flooring. I can still picture that kitchen, down a flight of stairs, in the basement. The room was long and narrow. The sink and stove sat at one end, beneath a ground-level window. To the left, a door opened to a furnace room that always gave off the smell of burnt dust. Flickering fluorescent lights colored the kitchen blue-gray, and cinder-block walls made it cold.

There was not much anyone could do to create beauty there.

But the grown-ups in my church figured out how, and it wasn't in the decorations.

An old man in the church volunteered to re-tile the kitchen floor. He bought the materials and went to work. Square linoleum tiles, ten by ten inches each. Half green and half brown, like a checkerboard. Whatever was on sale, I'm sure.

The old man glued down the tiles and went home, mission complete.

Later that day, two other men in my tiny church came to take a look. It was a disaster. The tiles were crooked. There were gaps all over the place. Glue oozed between the joints—this was in the day before peel-and-stick tile. The old man succeeded in making an ugly kitchen uglier.

This is the part of the story that put a lump in my young throat: The two men knew what they had to do. They called home and said they wouldn't make it to dinner. They rolled up their sleeves, peeled up the freshly laid tile, bought new tile and glue at their own expense, and re-laid the floor, nice and tight. It took them all night long. A whole night with no sleep, away from their families, and no dinner but fast food.

Here's the kicker: They never told a soul until years after the old man died.

My little-boy heart swelled with pride every time my Sunday school teacher told that story. These were great men. Yes, it was a simple thing—just a tile floor in a small church kitchen. No martyrdom. No grand gestures. But it was a beautiful thing.

No mirrors in sight.

They were ready for love. They were mature.

I've been loved like that. God surrounded me with good people who have loved me well. They were my Josephs. I hope they feel loved back by me. I'm sure there are plenty who have blessed me in ways I don't even know about.

In heaven, I'll thank them personally.

FOR REFLECTION AND DISCUSSION

1. Does it surprise you to think that Jesus endured the cross "for the joy" that was set before him? What do you think that means?

2. In your life, what has been the relationship between love and happiness?

3. Beyond your own needs and your own family, in what ways are you loving and serving others? What transcendent cause(s) have you seized?

4. Who has loved you well? Have you ever said thank you?

5. What does 1 Corinthians 13:11–12 say about the connection between spiritual maturity and love?

You Can Have
a Happy Life

God never made a promise that was too good to be true.

—D. L. Moody

✳ ✳ ✳

Ancient cultures often locked people into a fate they couldn't control. They were victims of monumental forces beyond their control. Some saw their destiny written in the stars. Others bowed to fickle gods with blessings for sale. A child born to a slave stayed a slave—never mind that child's genius or passion. Nature itself was a harsh mistress, as volcanoes, famines, and fires wreaked havoc in people's lives. Evil spirits threatened harm. Rival nations rattled sabres on insecure borders. People saw themselves as pawns of impersonal forces beyond their control.

For most, happiness was a luxury. A few fleeting moments here and there, maybe, but otherwise, life was a brutal ordeal of daily survival with random moments of pleasure thrown in.

The gods, the Fates, the stars, nature, famine, slave-masters, or the heel of oppressive government weighed on the human heart like a ball and chain on a convict.

Into that emotional dungeon, a follower of Christ named Peter dropped this bombshell . . .

> [Jesus], whom having not seen you love. Though now you do not see [Jesus], yet believing, you rejoice with joy inexpressible and full of glory . . .
>
> 1 Peter 1:8

Who writes stuff like that? "Joy inexpressible and full of glory."

Maybe, by temperament, you're a moody person. Maybe you see the half-empty side of the glass first. Life has been hard for you. People don't make sense, the world doesn't make sense, and you're caught in the middle.

I get you. My heart is with you.

I think Joseph would understand you too.

If he could fly back to earth and join us at Starbucks for lattes, I think his simple exhortation would be this: *You can have a happy life.*

You might stammer back, "Yes, b-but I lost my job, and my house is . . ."

"I'm sorry that happened," Joseph would say. "You can still have a happy life."

"But I'm an epic failure," you'd say.

"God has epic grace," he would whisper, swirling his drink with a biscotti.

"But I'm a little pawn in a vast cosmos."

"God has given you dominion," Joseph would say. "You reign. You are the captain of your fate. I'm telling you, you can have a happy life."

"But what about . . ."

His upraised hand would stop you. "I hear the pain in your voice." He might gently touch your hand or shoulder. "Life is too short to bow before the altar of adversity. I can promise you, there is no enemy so fierce, no pit so deep, and no prison bar so strong that it can block out God's gift of happiness, if you really want it."

You might smile and say, "So you won't allow me any excuses, will you?"

He might spout off in Egyptian or Hebrew.

"What's that?" you'd say.

"I just said, *Adversity is inevitable, but misery is optional*. It's my motto." He'd smile and add, "Plus, I've seen heaven. Believe me, you can have a happy life."

A moment of silence. A few sips of coffee.

Then, "Hey, there's a party tonight, and I think I'm late. Gotta run . . ." Joseph would take one more sip, give you a big hug Egyptian-style, and head for the door.

"Thanks," you would say.

Glancing over his shoulder, he'd say, "I'm counting on you. More people than you realize are counting on you."

And he'd be gone.

Now What?

But you're still here. What now?

Go get your happy life.

It's your birthright, your promised treasure from a heavenly Father who cheers every inch of ground you gain. A deeply happy life will not waft down to you from heaven. You will not stumble into it by accident.

You have to fight.

You have to fight to make the eleven secrets real.

You are in a war. The powers of darkness conspire to "steal, and to kill, and to destroy" your abundant life (John 10:10). Your own corruptions join the fray. You are in the arena, on the field of battle. Like a gladiator you must fight for your life. The angels cheer and the demons groan in dismay as you take your stand.

Who are the enemies?

Slay the dragon of *inertia*. Rouse yourself from apathy. Quit settling for second best. Jesus compared a lukewarm Christian to vomit (Revelation 3:16). Sorry. Stoke the fires of being whatever God called you to be. Wake up.

Behead the giant of *fear*. Everybody's afraid. Welcome to the club. I preach every week to a couple thousand people, and I get stage fright. Every single time. Plus, I'm an introvert by nature (it's official; I took a test). Maybe your fears are ten thousand times stronger, and mine seem minor by comparison. Okay. Remember this: *One plus God is always a majority*. When an old prophet found himself surrounded by the armies of the enemy, he told his assistant, "Those who are with us are more than those who are with them" (2 Kings 6:16).

If you're waiting for fear to go away, you'll be sitting in that rocker till a puff of air blows away your rotted corpse. Draw energy from your fear and hit the devil in the teeth.

This is your happiness we're talking about. No one can win it for you. Don't let fear stop you.

Rise above the swarms of *dysfunction*. Get whatever help you need. Recovery groups. Counseling. Treatment centers. Medicine. Prayer. Therapy. Marital counseling. No dysfunction, no addiction, no dependency can rule your life unless you roll over and play dead. Yes, sometimes we're held back by mental or emotional illnesses, or by chemical imbalances. God uses medicine. God uses doctors. Even the most sincere God-follower needs medical and medicinal help at times. I tell my church all the time, "Stay on your meds." Whatever issues you need to face, face them.

Don't be stuck in the same dysfunctions a year—or three or ten years—from now that you're stuck in today.

Stamp out those cockroaches and you'll almost hear the angelic stands go wild.

Crush your *immaturity* too. Spiritual immaturity is the problem lurking behind every other problem in your life. Grow up. Grow deep in God. Get out of spiritual kindergarten. Bible heroes like Joseph, Samuel, Daniel, Esther, and Mary (the mother of Jesus) rose to heroic heights as *teenagers*. They blew away their peers because early in life they pressed hard into God. "For though by this time you ought to be teachers, you need someone to teach you again the first principles of the oracles of God; and you have come to need milk and not solid food" (Hebrews 5:12).

Bible study, preaching, prayer, being in communion with God's people . . . those are basics, and there will never be a substitute.

What are you waiting for?

Above all, thrust a spear through the heart of *halfhearted devotion* to God. A broken-hearted woman in my church asked me for arguments against a false religion. Her daughter was marrying a man in that religion, she said, and she needed "arguments to prove the religion was wrong." I comforted her as much as I could. But in the end, I had to say her daughter's problem wasn't tolerance of a false religion, it was halfhearted devotion to God.

You have to decide who your God will be.

Joseph asked three questions: With a woman tugging his sleeve for sex, Joseph asked, "How can I sin against God?" With the golden opportunity to pump up his own standing, he asked, "Do not interpretations belong to God?" With means, motive, and opportunity to wreak vengeance upon his brothers, he asked, "Am I in the place of God?"

In each question, the presumed answer is *duh*.

He decided who his God was, and that gave him all kinds of clarity about who his God wasn't.

All those nasty forces within, raising their ugly heads to pull you back from obeying God, need to be put to death (Colossians 3:5).

You have not yet scratched the surface of the joy that can be yours. Step into your birthright. Go to war to gain your life. Wield the weapons of faith. Go on a campaign for deep happiness.

This is a fight you can win. God is with you.

He promised.

There is coming a day when all of heaven will raise a shout of praise in your honor—the humblest, most obscure follower of God, who refused to make even one more excuse for a lame, zombified half-life.

Going Home

And Joseph said to his brethren, "I am dying; but God will surely visit you, and bring you out of this land to the land of which he

swore to Abraham, to Isaac, and to Jacob." Then Joseph took
an oath from the children of Israel, saying, "God will surely visit
you, and you shall carry up my bones from here."

Genesis 50:24–25

Joseph saw future generations of Jews settling for Egypt's
half-life, and he worried for them. He feared they might be so
rooted in this alien land they would never return to their very
own Promised Land. So he made them swear an oath: *Bring my
bones back to the land of our fathers; make sure I get buried there.*

They were, in essence, swearing to get back to their spiritual
sweet spot.

Fast-forward. Four and a half centuries later, the Jews were still
in Egypt. They were no longer privileged guests of the Pharaoh.
They were slaves, flying beneath their dignity.

They remembered their Promised Land and cried out to God.
Way to go, Joseph, for planting that seed.

God sent Moses to set them free. The entire nation, two million strong, embarked upon an epic trek back to the Promised
Land. Guess whose bones they carried:

And Moses took the bones of Joseph with him, for he had placed
the children of Israel under solemn oath, saying, "God will surely
visit you, and you shall carry up my bones from here with you."

Exodus 13:19

Pilgrims in a Strange Land

For the person who follows God, this whole world is alien terri-
tory. Even your highest happiness is the faintest whisper of what's
coming. You are journeying to the land where "God will wipe
away every tear from [your] eyes; there shall be no more death, nor
sorrow, nor crying. There shall be no more pain, for the former
things have passed away" (Revelation 21:4).

In the end, heaven is God's ultimate, permanent, and most
open secret to happiness.

Child of God, your bones are going home.

You will swim in an ocean of joy in the presence of God, waves of happiness crashing upon you.

You will dive into delights so immense, earthly sorrows will fade into oblivion and earthly pleasures will seem like toddler games.

You will shine as a spectacle to dazzle the angels.

You will step into your fathomless inheritance, flashing an all-access pass to the vaults of heaven.

You will walk on streets of gold.

You will run to the arms of Jesus—your Savior, Deliverer, Champion, and Friend—for an embrace of overwhelming love.

You will join in the earsplitting applause for the absolute perfection of every twist and turn of providence.

You will raise a cheer to Jesus, grateful beyond words for the nail prints in his hands and feet—as inexpressible joy finds expression, and it's still not enough.

You will take your seat at God's table, for a feast to honor the One who is worthy of all glory, and honor, and praise.

Let the party begin. A party to end all parties. Pure joy. Infinite happiness.

You were made for this.

You can have a happy life.

PS, I'll race you to the dance floor.

FOR REFLECTION AND DISCUSSION

1. Can you have a happy life?

2. How confident are you of heaven?

3. How might confidence in heaven alter behaviors on earth?

4. What legacy of love might you send into the future long after you're dead?

5. Of the secrets to a happy life, which seem hardest to you? Easiest? Most unexpected?

6. How does 2 Corinthians 4:17 help set a person's adversity in an eternal context?

Acknowledgments

Publishing is a team sport, and God drafted me onto a good one. A big thank-you to my favorite and best teammate, my wife, Margi. I couldn't do this without your cheerleading, input, wisdom, and love. Josie and J.D., thank you for helping me understand what happiness means.

Thank you, Janet Kobobel Grant, for believing in me, and Tim Peterson for getting excited about this project. Jeff Braun's editorial expertise has been not only invaluable, but fun. Thank you, Brett Benson, for getting the word out. Nancy Bottom proofread and offered vital assistance. Author Dave Meurer dragged me into this whole adventure, and now I'm both hooked and grateful.

I am the product of five churches spanning a lifetime: Grace Gospel Church, North Side Gospel Center, Windy City Community Church, Grace Pointe Church, and now Neighborhood Church of Redding. Thank you all for giving me a family of faith and instructing me in God's Word.

Notes

Introduction: God Is Happy

1. D. Martyn Lloyd-Jones, *Spiritual Depression: Its Causes and Its Cures* (Grand Rapids, MI: Eerdmans, 1965), 109.

2. C. S. Lewis, *The Weight of Glory and Other Addresses* (Grand Rapids, MI: Eerdmans, 1965), 1–2.

What Is Happiness?

1. D. Martyn Lloyd-Jones, *The Life of Peace: Studies in Philippians 3 & 4* (London: Hodder and Stoughton, 1990), 208.

2. Jennifer Horton, "How Ocean Currents Work," How Stuff Works, accessed September 18, 2012, http://science.howstuffworks.com/environmental/earth/ocean ography/ocean-current3.htm.

3. Jeremiah Burroughs, *The Rare Jewel of Christian Contentment* (London: W. Bentley, 1651), 3.

4. Now dubbed The Stanford Marshmallow Study, www.sybervision.com /Discipline/marshmallow.htm.

Secret #1: Letting Go

1. Jack London, *The Call of the Wild* (New York: Grosset and Dunlap Publishers, 1903), 134.

Secret #2: Destiny

1. Here are all the uses of the word *report*: Numbers 13:32; 14:36, 37; Psalm 31:13; Proverbs 10:18; 25:10; Jeremiah 20:10; Ezekiel 36:3. Check them out for yourself. The Hebrew word is *dibbah*. The standard dictionary of biblical Hebrew offers these definitions: "whispering, defamation, evil report, unfavourable saying"

(*The New Brown-Driver-Briggs Gesenius Hebrew English Lexicon* [Peabody, MS: Hendrickson Publishers, 1979], 179).

2. G. R. Stephenson, (1967), "Cultural acquisition of a specific learned response among rhesus monkeys," in D. Starek, R. Schneider, and H. J. Kuhn (eds.), *Progress in Primatology* (Stuttgart: Fischer Verlag), 279–288, accessed September 12, 2012, http://wiki.answers.com/Q/Did_the_monkey_banana_and_water_spray_experiment_ever_take_place.

Secret #3: Consistency

1. All cited from Steven D. Mathewson, "An Exegetical Study of Genesis 38" in *Bibliotheca Sacra* 146 (1989), 373–392.

2. These early cultural and familial rules were enshrined in law many years later.

3. Helen B. Montgomery, *The New Testament in Modern English* (Elgin, IL: Judson Press, 1924).

4. Ephesians 4:19 (NIV1984).

5. William Barclay, *New Testament Words* (Philadelphia: Westminster Press, 1974), 234.

6. Ibid.

7. Ibid.

Secret #4: Loyalty

1. From his book, *Three Dollars Worth of God,* n.p., 1971.

2. This word *refused* with its accent indicates sustained struggle and steadfast refusal by Joseph.

Secret #5: Endurance

1. *The Oswald Chambers Devotional Reader* (Nashville: Thomas Nelson, 1990), 141.

2. Louis Berkhof, *Systematic Theology* (Grand Rapids, MI: William B. Eerdmans Publishers, 1996), 60.

Secret #6: Trust

1. "Domino Day Is Huge," Didn't You Hear, accessed March 1, 2013, http://didntyouhear.com/domino-day-is-huge/.

2. Weijers Domino Productions, Frequently Asked Questions, accessed March 1, 2013, www.dominodomain.com/FAQ-domino-room.

3. Weijers Domino Productions, Building Dominoes, accessed March 1, 2013, www.dominodomain.com/building-dominoes.

4. Louis Berkhof, *Systematic Theology* (Grand Rapids, MI: William B. Eerdmans Publishers, 1996), 165.

Secret #7: Closure

1. William Romaine, *The Life, Walk and Triumph of Faith* (London: James Clarke and Co., 1793), n.p.

Secret #8: Identity

1. John Owen, *Of Communion With God,* chapter 4, accessed March 5, 2013, www.iclnet.org/pub/resources/text/ipb-e/epl-09/owcom-05.txt.

2. Statistics from Awana's website, retrieved September 26, 2012. http://awana .org/about/about-awana,default,pg.html.

3. The Bible calls Christians "heirs of promise" (Hebrews 6:17); "heir of the righteousness" (Hebrews 11:7); and "heirs of the kingdom" (James 2:5). It calls Jesus the "heir of all things" (Hebrews 1:2)—where "all things" is the Greek phrase for the entire cosmos and all it contains. Then it calls us "joint heirs" with Christ (Romans 8:17). "Giving thanks to the Father who has qualified us to be partakers of the inheritance of the saints in the light" (Colossians 1:12).

4. Psalm 23:1; Genesis 22:14.

5. No less than Princeton theologian John Murray wrote, "Union with Christ is the central truth of the whole doctrine of salvation. . . . There is no truth, therefore, more suited to impart confidence and strength, comfort and joy in the Lord than this one of union with Christ." John Murray, *Redemption: Accomplished and Applied* (Grand Rapids, MI: Wm. B. Eerdmans, 1987), 170–171.

6. "I have been young, and now am old; yet I have not seen the righteous forsaken, nor his descendants begging bread" (Psalm 37:25).

7. Lewis Sperry Chafer, *Salvation: God's Marvelous Work of Grace* (Grand Rapids, MI: Kregel Classics, 1916), 59–65, and Chafer, *Systematic Theology*, Vol. III (Dallas: Dallas Seminary Press, 1948), 225–265.

Secret #9: Wisdom

1. Oswald Sanders, *Spiritual Leadership* (Chicago: Moody Press, 1967), 57.

2. R. Laird Harris, editor, et al., *Theological Wordbook of the Old Testament*, Vol. 1 (Chicago: Moody Publishers, 2003), entry #207.

3. C. S. Lewis, *The Weight of Glory and Other Addresses* (New York: MacMillan, 1949), 1–2.

Bill Giovannetti teaches at A. W. Tozer Theological Seminary and is senior pastor of the fast-growing Neighborhood Church. An experienced speaker and author, Bill seeks to inform the mind in ways that touch the heart. Known for his humor and down-to-earth delivery, he loves seeing people find their joy in God. Bill has been published in numerous magazines including *Focus on the Family*, *In Touch*, and *Leadership Journal*. This is his third book. His wife, Margi, an attorney, teaches at Simpson University. They are proud parents of two happy homeschooled kids. Learn more at www.BillGiovannetti.com or www.secretstoahappylife.org.